Design in Embroidery

Design in Embroidery

Kathleen Whyte

B. T. Batsford Limited
Charles T. Branford Company

To
Dorothy Angus and all my students

© Kathleen Whyte 1969
First published 1969
Reprinted 1970
Library of Congress Catalog Card Number 74-75770
7134 2633 0

Printed and bound in Great Britain by
Jarrold and Sons Limited, London and Norwich
for the publishers
B. T. Batsford Limited,
4 Fitzhardinge Street, London W.1 and
Charles T. Branford Company,
Newton Centre, Massachusetts 02159

Contents

Acknowledgment

To the Glasgow School of Art and students for willing permission to include photographs of work from the Embroidery Department, to former students for contributing photographs of their work, and to Messrs J. & P. Coats for kindly offering to supply photoprints of stitch diagrams. To Hannah Frew and Joan Jeffrey for photographing work and for help in other ways, to my sister for her valuable assistance in editing and typing the manuscript, and to other friends for their advice and encouragement.

K.W.   Glasgow 1969

Introduction

This book is offered to all who are interested in embroidery and design—to the novice, the worker with experience, and the student. It is intended as one side of a conversation in which readers are invited to take part, supplying further thoughts and ideas of their own.

There are so many ways of doing embroidery, and so many ways of thinking about it, that the word conjures up a wide range of images. To some people it can mean a satisfying pastime, while to others it can project itself as an art form, embracing a rich variety of creative activities and a constant challenge in design.

This is an analytical age, and we no longer think it sufficient to note that there are many kinds of embroidery, but find it necessary and also refreshing to enquire a little into the nature of the art itself, in order to discover all that goes into the making of one satisfactory example of any kind. A search reveals that this jewel—the excellent embroidery—has many facets for consideration, including the properties and handling of materials, ways of working, the practice of drawing, the nature of design, the use of colour, and being ingenious. All these play their part in creating a whole work, and are in practice completely involved together. Here, however, for the purpose of simple analytical thinking, each aspect is dealt with separately, and to avoid repetition, each section aims to keep exclusively to one topic. The various aspects are arranged in what seems to be a convenient sequence when thinking of embroidery and design in this logical way, but at times the order adopted may seem to create an unreal situation. For example, colour is found towards the end of the book; if a different cycle had been adopted, it might have been at the beginning, since it cannot be absent for long. Nothing is meant to be excluded at any point, but is, as it were, waiting in the wings. Finally, all aspects must be considered together.

At the beginning of each section an attempt is made to create an image of the subject under discussion; then to relate its function to embroidery; finally to present it to the reader as an 'opportunity'. This word seems to suggest graphically that the way is cleared for a new beginning, and each worker starting on a fresh pursuit.

This book is not intended to replace stitch books, nor those which deal with special techniques, but rather to complement them. A list of excellent reference books will be found at the end of the text.

With some exceptions, the illustrations represent a cross-section of work produced in the Embroidery Department of the Glasgow School of Art. Since the captions to the illustrations include the students' year of training, it could be noted that the Scottish system in Schools and Colleges of Art is slightly different from that pertaining to Dip.A.D. Colleges in England. Students attend for four years in the one Art School, spending two years in general art training, and thereafter specialising for two years in their chosen subjects. In effect, 'first year' in Scotland is equivalent to the 'foundation course' in England, and the Scottish 'fourth year' to the English 'third year Diploma in Art and Design'.

Teaching embroidery and design

Art is about values, and embroidery, like any other creative activity, provides a medium for training the senses to recognise them. It develops a textile sense—a feeling for fibres, yarns, and fabrics of all kinds; and a visual sense, attuning the eye to form, colour, and tone. It provides opportunities for discriminating choice, sharpening the critical faculty, and creating standards of quality, on which the worker learns to rely. It gives scope for ingenuity, but teaches restraint in that very quality, and the recognition that understatement can enhance the richest effect. Design is implicit in every part of doing embroidery: each stage of the creative process relies on a sense of proportion, pattern, and style.

Teaching endeavours to introduce these concepts to the student, with imagination and variety, creating a framework for individual development and a background for experiment, striking a balance always between giving formal instruction and inducing personal discovery. Teaching should enlarge a student's vision of her own potential; in the field of design it often consists in directing attention to the obvious.

At the present time the demarcation line between one form of expression and another is breaking down. Experiment abounds, and the concept of 'embroidery' has widened greatly—to include almost all inventive uses of threads and materials. New techniques will evolve to express new vision, but it is well to remember that the more an art form stretches out to experiment, and to become involved in the ideas belonging to other media, the more it is necessary for it to investigate its own foundations, so that, while receiving stimulus from outside, it may develop adventurously according to its own nature.

Historical review

Embroidery's historical past is like a large and fabulous tree with its roots nourished in many soils, producing on its branches colour, texture, and pattern characteristic of many ages and cultures. It can also be seen as an activity natural to all peoples, put to many uses, and rising at different times and in different places to an art of great vitality and beauty.

When, after hundreds of years, comparatively fragile creations of threads and stitches remain to astonish us by their excellence, time seems to stand still, and we are with those embroiderers of the past, sharing in their labours, marvelling at their skill, and imagining their intense satisfaction.

The functions of embroidery change. In the distant past its primary purpose was to enrich material, and that mainly for the adornment of kings, princes, and priests. It is in fact from the statues, illustrations, and writings of antiquity that we know of its existence in very early times. In the Book of Exodus there are detailed instructions for the making of Aaron's priestly robes—all in blue, of fine twined linen, with pomegranates of blue and purple and scarlet round about the hem, with bells of gold between them; the curtains of the tabernacle are also described—'with cherubims of cunning work'—and all done expressly 'for glory and for beauty'.

All magnificence is lacking in two extant fragmented roundels of Coptic embroidery,★ which seem to echo the spirit of early Christianity. On one, three figures stand, bound together by awe or grief, and on the other the Last Supper is depicted with a childlike simplicity. The work matches the subject-matter—completely simple and unaffected.

The Bayeux Tapestry shows embroidery as a recorder of historical events. It is probably the best-known piece of stitchery in the Western World, and certainly the most alive in design. It portrays dramatically the events which led to the Norman conquest of England, and has the topicality and excitement of a strip cartoon. It seems unique in its portrayal of secular events of that time—within twenty years of 1066. The workmanship though coarse is vigorous and accurate in drawing, losing nothing of the designer's original skill.

Opus Anglicanum, 'the fairest flower of English Gothic'—these are two names given to English ecclesiastical embroidery of the Middle Ages. This work was splendid in conception of design, figure drawing, and workmanship. Like the great stained-glass windows of the period, embroidery here

★ In the Victoria and Albert Museum, London

assumed an additional role and became a medium of instruction. Copes and chasubles, emblazoned with scenes from the Bible stories, helped to teach the people about religion. In a very practical sense craftsmanship at this time was directed to 'the honour and glory of God'.

In Elizabethan times embroidery adorned the State, helping to create the fantastically rich garments favoured by the Queen and her Court. One example will suffice to show how it could be used to transform quite ordinary material into something splendid. A stomacher of the period is worked in the characteristic scrolling stem design, enclosing pale silk flower heads and pea-pods, much loved by designers of this time. The shaded flower petals stand free, and the pods open to show small green peas. All are worked in the finest buttonhole stitch. The background is powdered with small steel spangles, and the effect is rich, fascinating, and ingenious—in fact, a complete transformation of unbleached cotton!

Time to sew, time to do embroidery, has always been a factor almost more impelling than fashion. To Mary Queen of Scots and her enforced hostess, Bess of Hardwick it was not only a pastime during the long imprisonment, but an absorbing occupation. In a letter, Mary wrote that she 'had to give over for very payne'. It is known that she sent for her limner to 'draw forth designs' for her, and it is more than probable that in all the examples that have been mentioned, with the possible exception of the Coptic roundels, the designing and the working of the embroidery were not by the same hand.

Every country from China to Peru can display its Court embroideries, and many have equally splendid peasant costumes, with techniques and traditions of design handed down from mother to daughter for generations, and worn on special occasions. This is embroidery for celebration and joyous display.

In each age the point of view changes, and with the advent of richly woven materials less embroidery was used on dress. It became in fact an accent, something to enhance lovely material; this is how it is used today, in much the same way as jewellery.

To follow the course of embroidery in the home would be to write a history of interior design, so large a part has it played in furnishing over the years. In the distant days of cold stone walls and hard wooden benches, it followed tapestry as a soft, warm covering to clothe these discomforts, and it was used as a means of creating magnificence in princely surroundings. Today museums display chair-seats, upholstery, and pillows, coverings for beds and tables, panels for walls, and many other articles from every period. They evoke the living conditions of those of past generations who could afford embroidery, and they provide a record of changing styles of design, as well as interesting techniques for the embroiderer to study.

Not only has fashion changed over the centuries, but the actual quality of work has fluctuated. Some periods display an excellent synthesis between inventive pattern-making and the ingenious use of stitchery, as instanced in the example from Tudor times, while in others a stagnation of ideas seems to have beset both designer and worker. This happened in the Victorian era, which saw embroidery applied in surfeit to countless domestic articles. Some of it was good, but some quite worthless, a mere monument to the doubtful virtue of being busy, feeling it necessary to produce, regardless of standards of design and taste.

The tea-table, that vision of elegance which seems best to epitomise the needlework of the Edwardian era, with its drawn thread work, lace, and silver, is now also a period piece along with the firescreen and the antimacassar. The modern interior is consciously planned for space, colour, and texture, presenting a wonderful opportunity for embroidery of this age to supply brilliant accents and textural features.

In this very brief review all the examples have illustrated some aspect of the use or intended purpose of embroidery in very different times and circumstances. Today, although wise application is always of the greatest importance, the general point of view has changed radically, and the main interest is focused on embroidery for its own sake. It is recognised as an art form of great sensitivity and scope, with something intrinsic to offer in the field of visual expression, something which no other medium can give. Now seldom the work of two people—designer and embroiderer—as in the past, it presents a wealth of opportunity for individual experiment and creation.

This change has come about gradually, owing much initially to movements such as that of William Morris, and Art Nouveau, during which embroidery in common with all the crafts acquired fresh impetus and a new dignity through the reawakening of good design. Since early in the present century it has taken its place in schools and colleges of art throughout this country, and has developed as an increasingly important subject in the design field.

Embroidery from the past is recognised by design, characteristic of its period. Today, design fashion in general moves rapidly, and no one style can be taken for long as typical of a period. Curving action has replaced static form, and textural effect given way to hard edged shape. These popular expressions stem from the general trend in art to probe and investigate chosen areas of the whole design field. This, with an urge to reassess existing art forms and explore the possibilities of new media and materials is what characterises the present age.

A general outward-looking and at the same time self-regarding attitude provides a healthy stimulus to all forms of expression, embroidery no less than any other. It need never be confined by tradition, nor any accepted style, but should seek continually, within the compass of good design, to add its own true statement to the art of every age.

1 *Thick yarns: string, fishing-line, sisal, polypropylene,
raffia, etc.*

Threads

Embroidery is made of threads. This obvious statement has wide
implications, for 'thread' can be taken as a comprehensive term to mean:

all embroidery threads in cotton, linen, silk, wool, and rayon;
all manner of strings and twines in linen, hemp, jute, and cotton;
thongs, laces, hairs, and fibres;
weaving yarns, from coarse hand-spuns to gossamer synthetics;

2 *Finer yarns: linens, hemp, cottons, rayons, silk, wools,*
metallic yarns, Japanese gold, etc.

all knitting and crochet wools, yarns and mixtures, including metallic
and lurex threads;
Japanese golds and silvers, also purls, plates, and cords;
reels of machine threads, buttonhole twists, and waxed linens;
polypropylene, plastics, and other synthetics—

in fact, anything which will make a stitch, including yarns taken from the
background material or from other fabrics (*1, 2*).

3 *Thread drawing on paper from landscape, shows a variety
of yarns in use*   Margaret McLellan, Third Year

It is impossible to instance every kind of yarn. They are all prepared for
specific purposes. Their variety is vast, due to the diversity of their raw
materials, and also to the individual ways in which they are prepared and
spun. Their characteristics differ enormously. Their surfaces have different
textures—supple smoothness of silks, shininess of rayons, hairiness of wools,
and the more brittle quality of synthetics. Their bulks and twists make them
behave differently; a tightly twisted yarn has a wilful, springy quality (*17*),
while floss silk and soft wool, which have very little twist, spread and cover
the surface easily.

Embroidery can use them all. Each one makes a different statement on
material. Each is already a type of line and can be used to draw (*3*), creating
many variations. They ask to be used differently. They can be split, used
whole, or combined in groups to form multiple strands giving wide variety
in scale and texture.

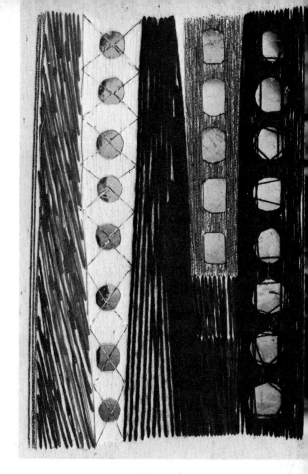

4 Long straight stitches in wools, rayons, and embroidery cottons, in shades of green, turquoise, and white, used as complete contrast to shisha glass (a type of mica from Kashmir, widely used in Indian embroidery)

5 Brightly coloured threads make line patterns converging on a centre of plastic shapes and sequins. See also 70
Joan Jeffrey, Post Diploma

6 Experimental string panel
Second Year

7 and 8 Two details from a string construction showing linen yarns, weaving, and plaiting
Hannah Frew, Third Year

9 Small hanging on fine garden net, using various kinds of yarn in white and silver, to discover methods of filling a fragile base   *Agnes Hamilton, Fourth Year*

10 Experiment after seeing a Mexican votive board which is made by pressing yarn into beeswax-coated hardboard. Knotting and felt background are departures from the original technique   *Joan Jeffrey, Post Diploma*

Opportunity in threads

Become interested in threads.

Collect them.

Every yarn which passes through your hands adds to your textile experience.

Examine their qualities and consider what they can do for you.

Use them in quite unconventional ways, with or without a background—tying and knotting, for instance.

Sew them in long stitches into a firm background, comparing their line qualities and how they look together.

Regard the whole enterprise as something new, and be prepared to consider favourably quite primitive effects in your search for new ways of working.

Learn to think in threads.

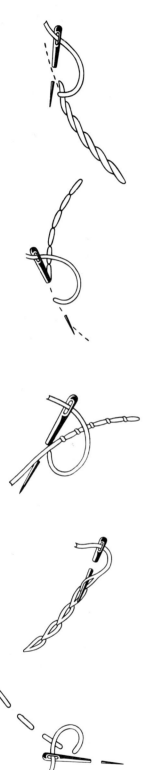

Stitches

Primitive man, sitting at his tent door, thonging skins together, liked the look of his stitches and decided to do another row—just for fun, for his own satisfaction. Thus embroidery must have been born—out of domestic need.

Stitches are ways of using threads. Embroidery stitches are ways of enhancing the varied qualities of threads (*12*). Conventions in using threads have grown up in different countries over the centuries, many stitches still being called after their place of origin, such as Roumanian stitch, Cretan stitch, and Pekinese stitch. The collection of known stitches is very large and varied; it is international, although many of the names differ from country to country. It has come to be known as 'stitchery', and is the embroiderer's alphabet.

Dictionaries of stitches are fascinatingly full of possibilities. Learning to make stitches, like learning to spell, is a simple skill, but it requires practice and ingenuity to find out how best to make use of them. Each stitch has its own character (*13*), but this varies when worked on different fabrics, or with different yarns, or by varying the size and tension. It is, in fact, well-nigh impossible to exhaust the vast potential of any one stitch. First stitches in embroidery are all-important, for it is here the worker lays a good foundation for the future, discovering the relationships which exist between threads, stitches, and background.

At this early stage it is wise to choose simple grounds such as hessian, coarse linens, and evenly woven furnishing fabrics, which are firm but open, and make good bases for displaying the qualities of threads and the effects of stitches. Woollen dress materials, such as hopsacks and flannels, are sympathetic and pleasant to handle; they make good foundations for wool embroidery. Gradually experiment shows that fabric with definite characteristics modifies the choice of yarns, and as the worker becomes sensitive in handling materials she enjoys finding the right threads for each different type of fabric.

Starting off with a suitably varied selection of yarns, it is quite a good plan to begin working with a thread rather like the background in size and texture, and from this norm to choose others, both thicker and thinner, which will provide variety as they are worked into the ground. Yarns which have a bold impact when seen in hanks and skeins undergo a complete change on being sewn stitch by stitch into material. The process is slow, but

11 Line stitches: stem, back, couching, split, and running

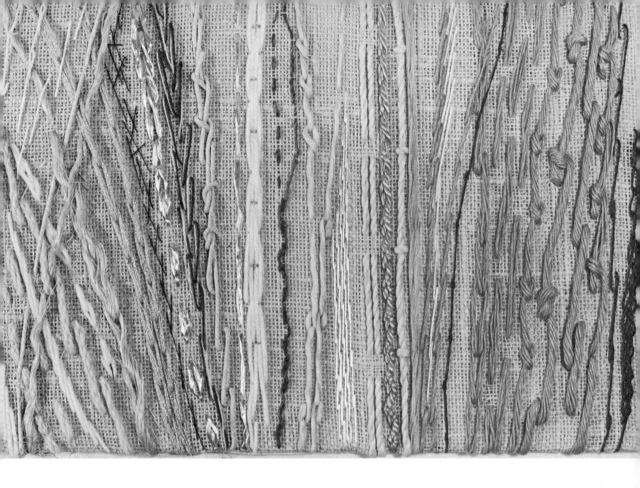

12 Threads into stitches: very simple line stitches worked on heavy linen scrim display the varied qualities of a number of yarns—cotton, linen, and sisal strings (some split), multistrands of fine wool and lurex, waxed linen, raffene, knitting nylon, and embroidery silk. Stitches: variants of running, stem, split, and chain

13 Stitches in natural rhythm, yarn and stitch complementing each other

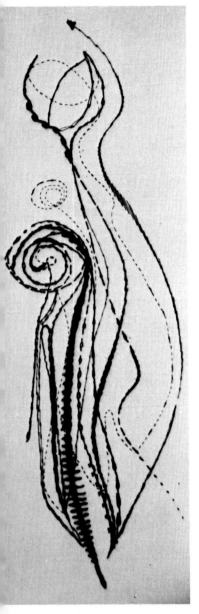

interest in what each stitch can do (*18*), curiosity to see the effects made by unfamiliar threads, and sufficient imagination to see the material 'embroidered' sustain the worker. Embroidery can suffer from being too 'thin' (not enough body to it), or conversely 'overwrought' (congested looking); finding the ideal quality is the very foundation of good embroidery.

The actual link between thread and fabric is of course the needle. Having a good selection of needles is important, and with even a little experience, a sensitive worker will feel quite unable to use a needle which is wrong for a particular job. The eye of the needle must be large enough to take the thread comfortably and make an adequate hole for its passage through the material. The action of pulling thread through fabric should be pleasant. There is, after all, a sensuous satisfaction in the sheer mechanical act of stitching. There are three types of needle—*crewel*, which is long, slim, and pointed, with a long eye for fine threads; *chenille*, which is thick and pointed, with a very large eye for thick threads; finally, the *tapestry* needle, which is like the chenille, but blunt, for canvas work.

Stitch books perform the useful function of arranging stitches in categories, according to their nature and use. It is only necessary here to elaborate a little on the functions of the main groups.

Line stitches Everyone is familiar with stem, back, chain, and running stitches (*11*), worked regularly in lines, but all such stitches can also be used for free drawing, and are fascinating as variable lines, constantly changing their density from strength to delicacy, and moving in curves and loops with ease and fluidity (*14a*). The several varieties of chain stitch can be made to slip easily from one to the other (*16*), creating a free pattern line, and there are also certain pairs of stitches, such as heavy chain and vandyke (*14b*), which have an ability to grow one from the other. Stitches used in this way have the quality of handwriting, and the worker will soon acquire her own style.

14a Fine-line sampler shows variety in line by changing from one stitch to another, using several weights of black thread on medium linen. 7″ × 18″. See also 72a and 76

Repeating lines Repeating rows of line stitches is one of the easiest ways of filling a space or creating an area, and the quality of the stitch is greatly enhanced in this way (*15*). A flat stitch, such as stem, can create a smooth satin-like surface, and if the direction of the working changes frequently, facets of varied reflection are created (*Plate 7*). Exact geometrical shapes may ask for regular and precise fillings, while vague shapes can have more casual treatment. Following this general line of thought, contrasting stitches can obviously be repeated in endless combinations of selected groupings to make all kinds of surfaces, smooth, ridged, and rough.

Building stitches Stitches like Cretan, herringbone, chevron, buttonhole, and fly have very individual formations, and are peculiarly suitable to use as design units (*19, 20, 21*). They build and link together easily, and can create formal patterns of a geometric nature, or when used freely tend to develop individual rhythms in characteristic shapes (*13, 18, 34*).

Knotted stitches Spanish knotted feather, rosette chain, knotted cable chain, French knot, and double knot—are all textural stitches, and introduce the element of depth into embroidery (*22a*). They make areas resembling astrakhan and strange knitting, and are particularly effective when worked with a multiple thread—perhaps wools in closely related tones of a colour, with a shiny thread to give occasional highlights to the texture (*22b*).

Decorative lines Composite stitches—those which need more than one step to complete—such as Pekinese stitch, sheaf stitch, raised chain band, and interlacing stitch, have a beautifully formal character, and when worked with smart, corded threads can be used very effectively as simple dress decoration (*24b*).

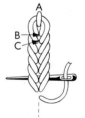

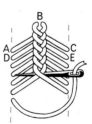

14b Heavy chain and vandyke stitch

15 Repeating lines for simple space filling. Red ground worked in orange, reds, and purple. Stitches: stem, split, and couching. 12″ × 5″. See also Plate 7

Elise Curr, Third Year

16 Chain, twisted chain, and cable chain stitches

17 Linen sampler, showing quality and behaviour of ▶ various linen yarns, thick rough-spun to hard waxed threads on linen paper

16

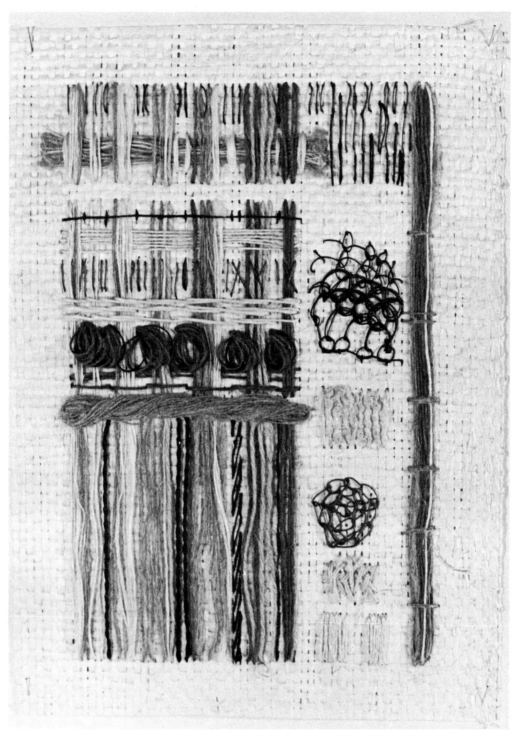

17

18 Stitch areas. Shape evolves from the nature of stitch worked in well chosen threads. Roumanian builds in blocks with easily packing wool; French knots grip and sparkle in wool and linen used together; erratic twisted chain behaves well in tightly spun rayon; mohair filling lies on the surface of the material, etc. Hessian ground

19a Small panel, 10″ × 8″, built on fly stitch variations. Black thread on white, with accents of colour. See also 73
Catriona Leslie, Third Year

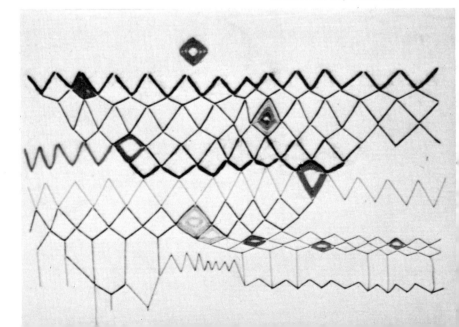

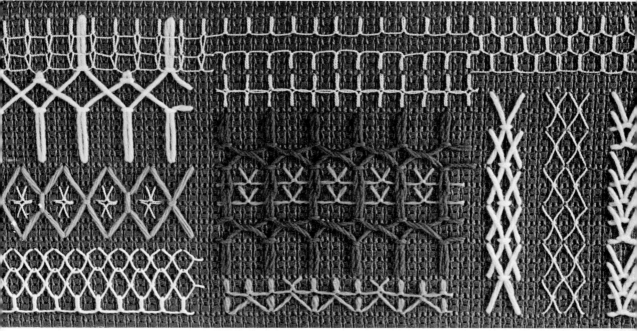

20a Up-and-down buttonhole one-stitch sampler. This stitch has great versatility as a pattern-building unit of design, and foundation for elaborate work. See also 111

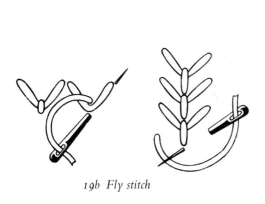

19b Fly stitch

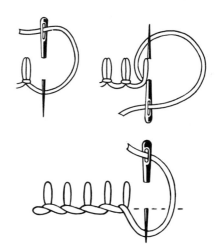

20b Up-and-down buttonhole and buttonhole stitches

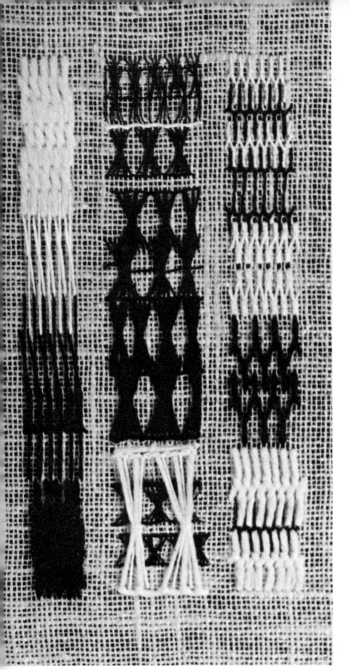

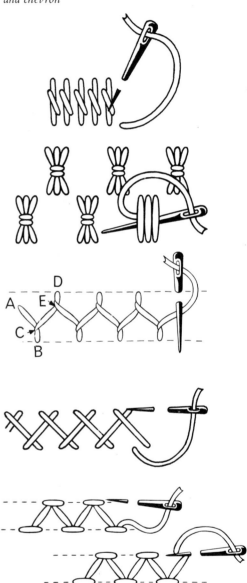

21b Building stitches: Roumanian, sheaf, Cretan, herring-bone, and chevron

A
D
E
C
B

21a Variation on a stitch. Roumanian, sheaf, and Cretan stitches worked by the thread of the material. Interest achieved by varying thickness and tone of threads, and by changing the size of the stitch. (See Opportunity in techniques, page 61)

a Knotted stitches: French knot, double knot, knotted
le chain, rosette chain, Spanish knotted feather, and
rtuguese stem

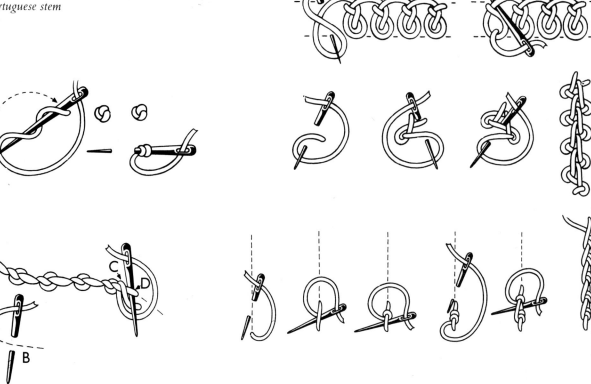

22b Detail of deep texture panel, 12″ square. Pinks,
orange, magenta, and purples on a flame woollen ground.
Area first broken by freely worked Cretan stitch; arrangement of colour carried out in French knots, using various
thicknesses and mixtures of woollen yarns, with highlights
in pink, mauve, and yellow raffene
See also 31 and 119a   Margaret Allan, Fourth Year

23 Ideas for using building stitches to make decorative
circles. Designs by young students working to a time limit
of one hour. See also 113. Photograph: courtesy Facet,
Glasgow School of Art   G. Huntly, Design Course

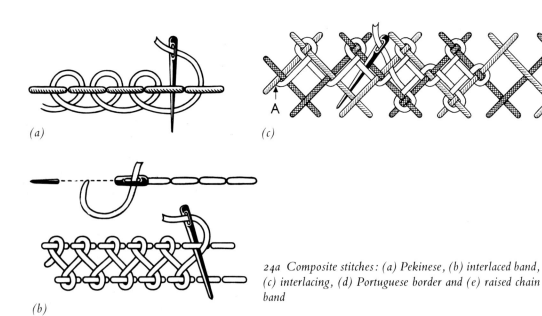

24a Composite stitches: (a) Pekinese, (b) interlaced band,
(c) interlacing, (d) Portuguese border and (e) raised chain
band

(d) C↗ ↖↑ B
    A

(e)

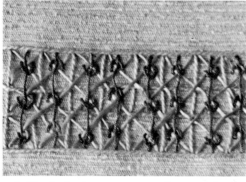

24b Simple border patterns on dress weight materials, using more than one stitch. Roumanian threaded, and lattice fixed with long-legged chain

24c Sampler of composite stitches on straw cloth in raffene and lurex cord

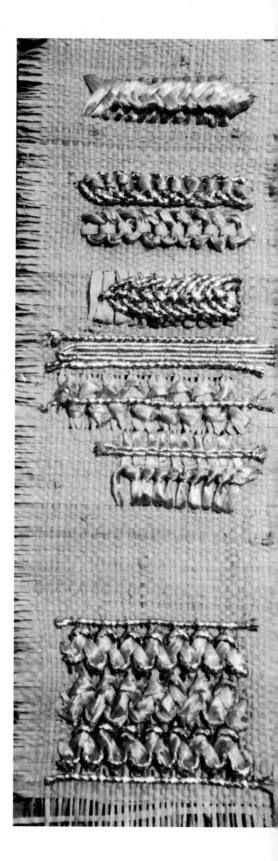

25 Stitches: scroll, closed buttonhole, closed feather, loop, feather, and open chain

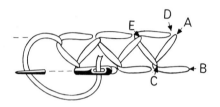

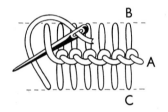

Opportunity in stitches

SAMPLERS

A sampler is a practice piece—a try-out for any kind of embroidery, in the first instance to learn how to work the stitches, then to investigate their possibilities, and finally to try effects before embarking on a large work. There have been samplers in all periods of embroidery, and it is unfortunate that the word has become too closely associated with the Victorian cross stitch variety.

Have a varied collection of threads, a selection of simple background materials, a good stitch book, and suitable needles.

ONE-STITCH SAMPLERS

Choose a line stitch and work it on a suitable background in a number of different yarns to compare the variety of scale and texture effects which can be obtained, first as free line, and then by repeating lines closely as surface texture. Try out various line stitches in this way.

EXPERIMENT

Experiment with different stitches, singly and together, on various background materials; change the scale of working by using thick and thin threads; change the tension and regularity. Work freely, and attempt to develop new relationships between threads and background by your use of stitches.

Use building stitches in simple logical ways to make basic patterns—up-and-down buttonhole, chevron, Cretan, etc.

Make stitch areas, choosing threads such as corded rayons, floss silks, wools, and machine threads, and using whichever seems to suit the characteristics of each particular stitch. Some stitches enjoy thick multiple strands made by combining different yarns. Experiment to find mixtures of yarns that will enhance the appearance of suitable stitches.

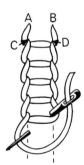

Make texture samplers to explore the possibilities of knotted stitches.

Use composite stitches on evenly woven material, and choose threads with care to produce smart decorative effects.

Doing embroidery

Doing embroidery is a gradually evolving process. As the worker experiments with threads and gains experience, knowledge of stitchery grows, and through using it, judgement and sensitivity develop. This introduces the very important thought, that there are two aspects in all creative activity—on the one hand, ways of working, methods, the mechanics of doing the job; on the other hand, something which is much more difficult to define, namely that which creates 'quality', compounded of choice and judgement—in fact, the aesthetic part. To appreciate this dual endeavour right from the start is to avoid the mistaken thought that methods or techniques alone are sufficient, and to realise that there is much more to discover. At first, choice and judgement are quite instinctive, and, in a sense, to be a true reflection of personality, they must remain so, but gradually they become informed, educated, influenced by design thought. In the exploration so far, design has actually made a start, in the thoughtful choice of yarns, and in the selecting of stitches. These are conscious and deliberate acts towards designing.

The following examples of student exercises illustrate how, from these early steps in choice and discrimination, the instinctive feeling for design can develop through doing embroidery. Six exercises were carried out by a class of thirty first year girls in ten three-hour periods. The large majority of the students had done no embroidery previously.

Background Canvas paper, 15″ × 12″.
Threads A very large selection of natural yarns from which to choose.
Brief Make a selection of threads, and do any kind of stitching on the background, to see what the threads look like when sewn (*26*).

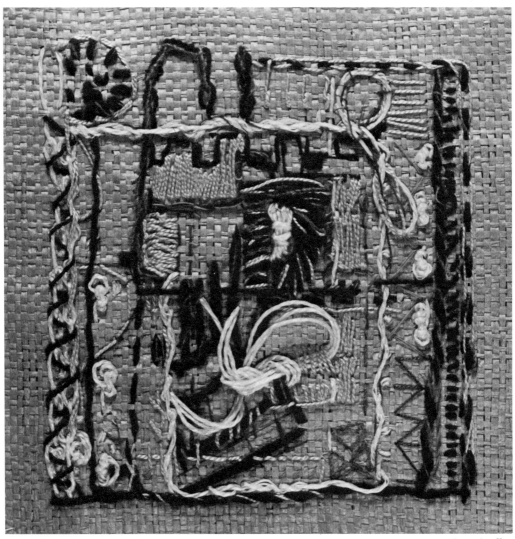

26a Strives for rich effect

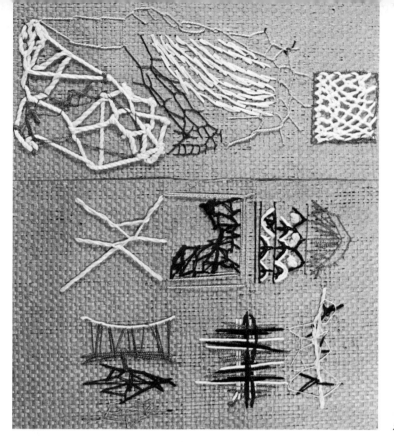

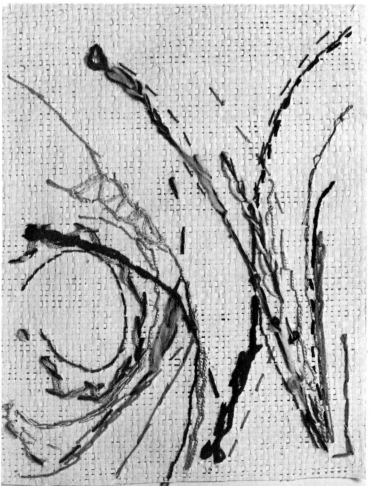

26b and c Exploring

26d Purposeful

EXERCISE 2

Background and Threads   Similar to Exercise 1.
Simple stitch book to consult.
Brief   Make vertical lines of stitches, choosing freely from the book.
Study the effects made by the various threads when they become stitches
(*27*).

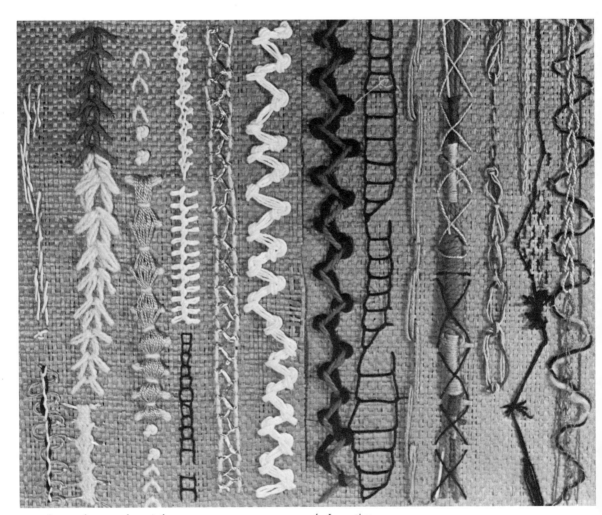

27a *Attracted to complex stitches*   27b *Inventive*

27c Good variety in scale of yarns　　　　　*27d Orthodox, with well balanced tone*

EXERCISE 3
Background Hessian—choice of colour.
Threads Linens and coton perlé in strong colours.
Stitches Cretan and up-and-down buttonhole stitch were demonstrated, and an element of freedom suggested.
Brief Make a piece of stitchery resembling 'network' (*28*).

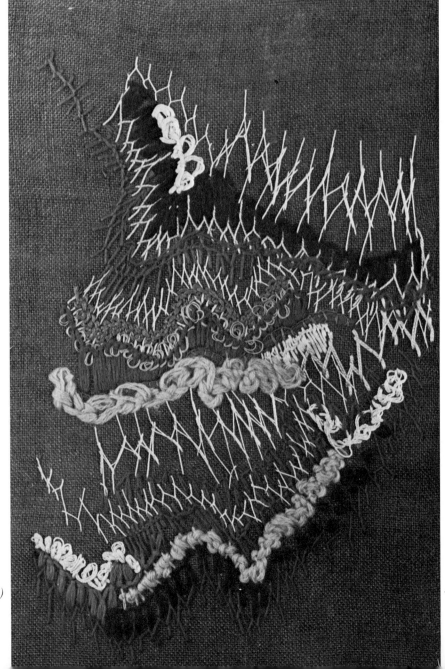

40   (*a*)

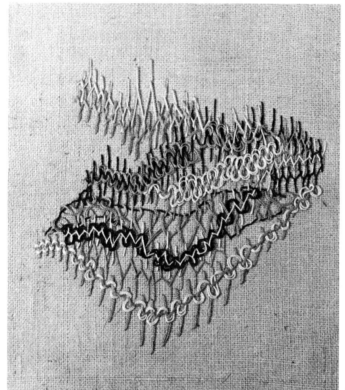

(b)

(c)

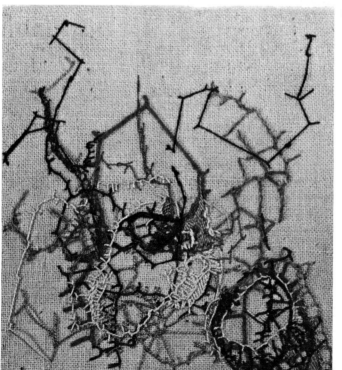

EXERCISE 4

Background　Hessian.

Threads　Much larger variety in colour.

Brief　Make an embroidery from the idea of 'strata'. (This proved an excellent starting-point, in that it suggested a simple design formation, with possibilities for variety in size and use of stitches.) (*29*.)

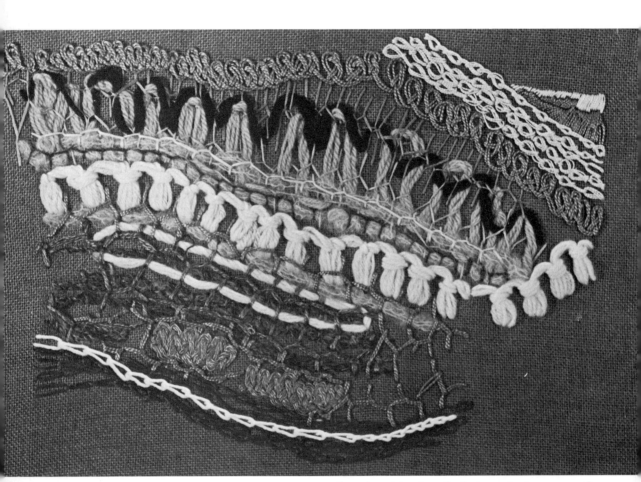

29a On coloured hessian, displaying quite joyous use of colour. Good varied use of stitches

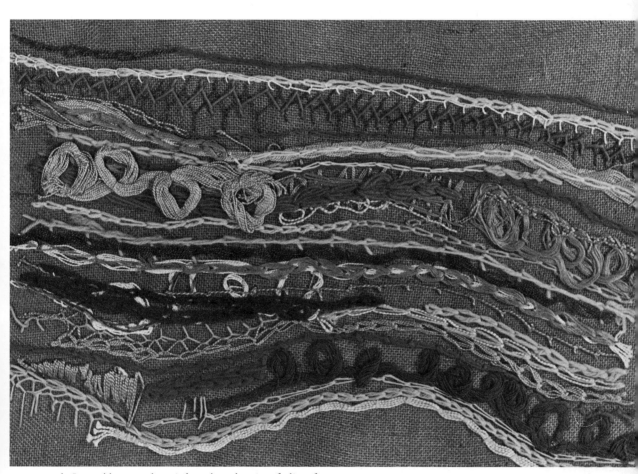

29b Less able to make stitches, but showing feeling for threads and design

30 *Precision not requested in this exercise. Work appears to be more 'on' the background than 'with it', in spite of regularity of weave. See also 32*

EXERCISE 5
Background Nubby linen scrim.
Threads Free choice in colour and kind.
Brief Make bands of pattern, having considered the idea that stitches are pattern-forming units. (It was suggested that organisation might be fairly neat, but there was no compulsion to count the threads of the material.) (*30*.)

EXERCISE 6
Backgrounds and Threads Own choice.
Brief Make an embroidery from the idea of 'varied textures' (*31*).

Discrimination, invention, taste, and the ability to handle texture and colour—all these qualities were apparent to a greater or lesser degree. Although the overall level of achievement was high, and the work spontaneous, all students did not excel in the same way, and only a few produced consistently good results throughout the six exercises. One, who had made three fairly poor attempts, suddenly produced a splendid 'Strata', indicating that, although she had very little ability to sew, the subject created an image for her, and inspired her to use threads roughly but effectively.

This series of exercises served to break down preconceived ideas about embroidery, and to create confidence in tackling a new subject. The students learned that the most successful results followed from a rich and full use of yarns, enterprising choice of stitches well spaced on the background, and a feeling for brilliant colour, while inability to handle material, a conservative choice of yarns and colour, congested stitches in small areas, and poor use of space—produced unsatisfactory effects.

These results illustrate in a small way the diversity of ability found in any group of beginners, and what can be achieved with a minimal amount of guidance. The way can be cleared for them; methods can be taught; problems can be aired and discussed. The best way to learn is by experience and personal discovery, for things learned in this way are peculiarly one's own.

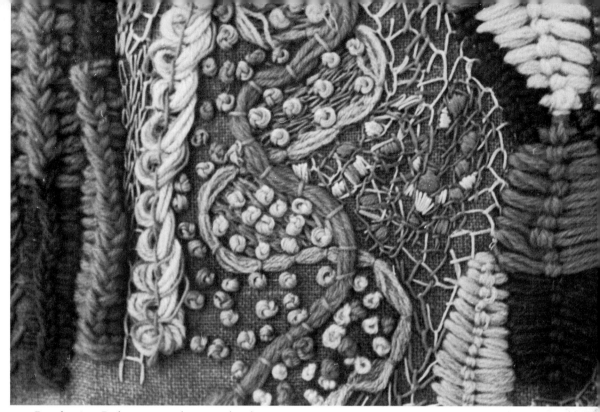

31a *Rust hessian. Red, orange, and green embroidery*

31b *Pink, mauve, and white on wine-coloured ground*

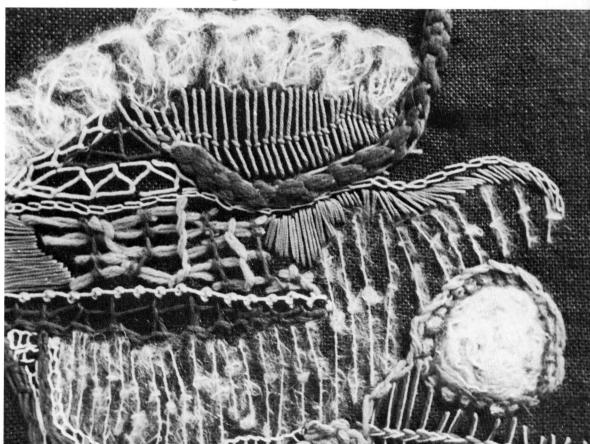

32 More conventional sampler on linen, worked with Anchor soft embroidery cotton, Knox's linen thread, and stranded cotton, in red, pink, and orange. Well chosen and organised blocks of stitchery and colour. Compare with preceding exercises

Opportunity in doing embroidery

In carrying out the exercises as described above, increase your knowledge of stitches, and develop your own ideas for combining them. (When working stitchery do not plan too far ahead. Proceed from what you feel to be right and the next step will become apparent from the 'look' of what has been done.)

Technique

This is a suitable point at which to look at the word 'technique', and to examine the various shades of meaning which it has acquired.

The dictionary defines it as—'everything concerned with the mechanical part of an artistic production'—the method, the way of working. Stitchery itself can be called a technique, and we also speak of 'traditional techniques' of embroidery. These may be very specialised, as in gold work (46), or have historical or foreign origins, as in black work and Hardangar. Drawn thread, drawn fabric (42–45), and other types of white embroidery are included, as well as canvas work and patchwork (35, 39). Each of these is a specialised area of practice with its own materials and methods. The fact that all traditional techniques have been practised over long periods, in some cases for generations, and almost always among groups of workers, has perfected their methods and raised them at times to high skills with amazing standards of technical proficiency, which cannot be attempted by most workers today.

Museums provide many examples of this kind of intricate work, and readers will be able to recall examples they have seen. Ayrshire 'Flowering' is one. Christening robes, caps, collars, and cuffs in very fine white embroidery on fine cotton lawn, with incredibly intricate needle-point insets, were produced as a cottage industry during the first half of the nineteenth century. In this instance, as in others, the workers were highly trained to execute prepared designs. Skill was their stock-in-trade, but only to a limited degree were they creative. Today people say in admiration, 'Isn't the technique marvellous!' Technique here means accomplished workmanship, and this is always worthy of high praise, but it must be borne in mind that skilful working is only one facet of embroidery, and if unaccompanied by some ability to design, is rather a sterile virtue.

Values and standards to excite admiration change in different periods. Today the accent is on discovery, self-expression, and experiment— daunting words to the beginner, but, as has been shown, everything starts modestly, and a worker using stitches well in her own way may be described as having an 'original technique'. This implies more than actual mechanical doing; it suggests that a personal quality has developed—an original approach in using stitches.

In an experimental period work does tend to be larger in scale and more rapid in execution. Today 'a good technique in stitchery' does not imply precision, but the quality of good drawing in thread, with spontaneity, assurance, and rhythm (*34, 161c*). It no longer seeks a mechanical perfection, but is imaginative, saying personal things with threads, and it is impossible to separate this activity from design. It is design which grows under the worker's fingers—organic design. A word of caution here—just as neatness and precision are no longer sufficient cause for admiration, neither is cleverness alone, and today's experimental methods of working demand their own high standard of accomplishment. It is part of their technique to present a professional quality.

Special and traditional techniques

Many opportunities for experiment exist within the specialised areas of embroidery, but it is outwith the intention of the present study to do more than draw attention to a few of these. Some offer more scope for invention than others, but most are characterised by a close link between technique and design, the most suitable type of design being suggested by the established way of working. It follows that the clue to invention is found in each case in the technique itself, in the simplest basic practice and idea behind the work.

PATCHWORK offers such opportunities (*35, Plate 1*). With its method of joining together straight edges of material to make a new fabric, it is a splendid technique for geometric design, allowing the present-day worker to express herself boldly in a modern idiom, while still working in the same manner as the creators of the original patchwork quilts, whose traditional design and ageless charm she can still appreciate.

CANVAS WORK embraces several techniques and has such a variety of methods and effects that it is difficult to pin-point any one common objective, unless it be simply to 'fill' the canvas in a satisfactory manner, using in the first instance very simple stitches, and arriving at the right density of threads to make a compact and durable material suitable for chair-seats, bags, and rugs (*Plate 1*). Tent stitch, Florentine, and various other stitches belong exclusively and traditionally to canvas work, but the

Plate 1 Three cushions in simple canvas stitchery. 'Liquorice All-sorts' design in patchwork   Third Year

33 Cushions. Two in white wool with coloured stitchery are soft and fleece-like; others show free 'painterly' embroidery, and one is formal in design

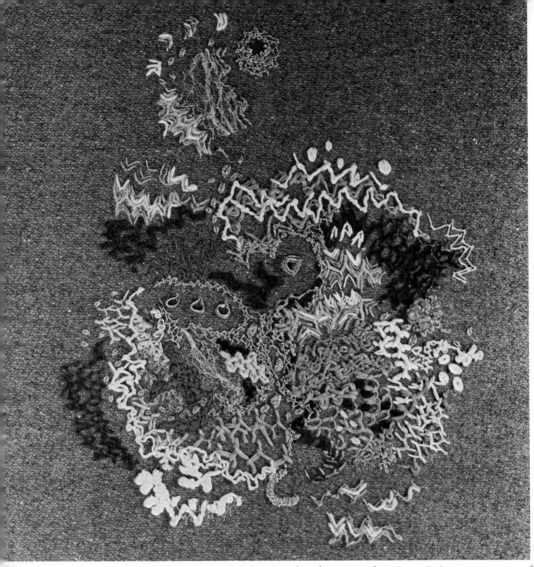

34 Panel on brown wool, 20" × 24", in an assortment of natural coloured threads and gold, seems to illustrate the idea of an easy rhythmical technique. See also 76 and 161
Catriona Leslie, Third Year

student will find that almost any stitch from the regular vocabulary has interesting possibilities on canvas, particularly when a variety of yarns is used to enhance the textural quality of the work (39). Canvas work, with its emphasis on regularity in working, can provide plenty of scope for experiment in geometrically controlled design—in other words, for arrangements of simple directional effects of stitches achieved by counting threads and spaces in the canvas (36). As in other specialised areas, it is not necessary to make a very comprehensive study of stitches before beginning to experiment and work in an individual way. In fact too much conformity to tradition can be cramping to invention; it is sufficient to master some basic practices.

35 Patchwork cushion. Black and white poplin in 'Op Art' arrangement of diamonds and triangles

Hannah Frew, Third Year

(Plate 1 shows another patchwork cushion with 'Liquorice All-sorts' design, evolved through manipulating actual sweets)

36a Canvas work cushion in tan and white wool. Directional stitchery creates a play of light in the design seen against a static white background of brick stitch

Sara Colquhoun, Fourth Year

36b Detail

36a

36b

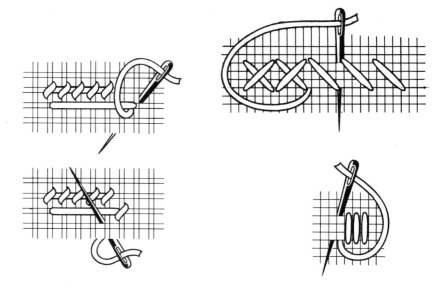

37 *Three simple canvas stitches: tent, cross, and satin*

38 *Union Jack cushion. Flag used as a design motif in red, white, and blue. The colours grow softer as the flags decrease in size. Various simple canvas stitches employed against a ribbed ground   Fiona McGeachy, Fourth Year*

(a)

(b)

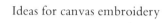

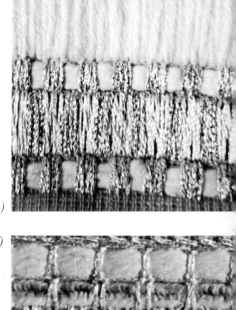

(e)

(f)

Ideas for canvas embroidery

39a Heavy canvas. Roumanian stitch in tightly packed groups of natural and brown camel hair, threaded with white rug wool

39b and c Pattern-making with straight stitches (satin) in brightly coloured wools

39d Variation on Florentine embroidery. Black wool, silver yarn, and white rayon

39e Border in white nylon, cream wool, rayon, and silver

39f Up-and-down buttonhole stitch in silver knitting yarn couches turquoise nylon and confetti chenille

39g Pattern darning on even-weave furnishing material: detail from 114

(c)

(d)

(g)

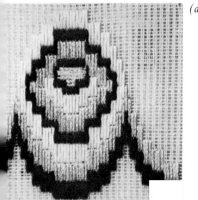

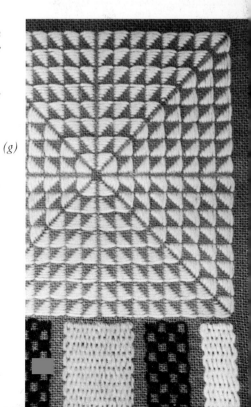

OPEN-WORK TECHNIQUES, such as drawn thread work and drawn fabric, aim mainly at changing the structure of the material and enriching the basic cloth by transparent effects, by making holes of many shapes and sizes, slits and open-work effects in great variety of pattern. Traditionally these techniques are worked on evenly woven material 'by the thread', and there are extensive collections of special stitches by which the material is transformed into open-meshed and lace-like structures. As the names imply, there are two basic practices: either threads are withdrawn completely from the material, making initially ladder-like effects (43), or the square construction of the material is distorted by pulling its threads together in bunches, and tying them with stitches (44). These ideas can be used as starting-points from which to develop new ways of working, for although the techniques are used traditionally to enrich domestic articles, they have great decorative possibilities, particularly in the field of transparent embroidery (42, 45).

Mention of even-weave material and working 'by the thread' highlights the contrast between the precise nature of working associated with some of these traditional techniques, and the spontaneous; rhythmical work in favour today. These two qualities, formality and freedom, are encountered throughout all art: both are important, and each has its own use. Some workers incline more readily to one way of working, and some to the other; some revel in free expression and find it rather inhibiting to work neatly and exactly, and others love to sew with prized regularity and cannot bring themselves easily to a more spontaneous approach. Possibly these two ways of working, regular and free, represent two aspects of personality, and the development of both should be encouraged.

40a

40 *Evolving a new technique. Two cushions of heavy cream woollen hopsack embroidered in several weights of black wool. Design suggested by lace. In (a) strands of heavy corded wool are fixed at the top; in (b) they are fixed to a ring at the centre. These are knotted in pairs and groups, and periodically fixed to the background. The pattern spreads down from the top in (a), and grows from the centre in (b). Further stitchery added to complete the designs*   Kathleen Whyte

40b

41 *Fine silk stitchery on wool*

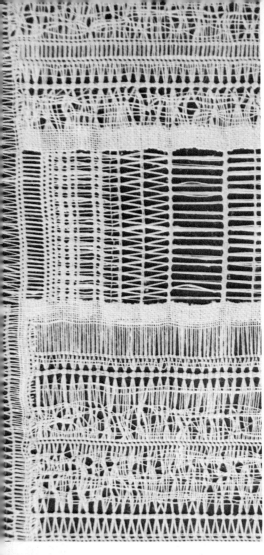

(a)

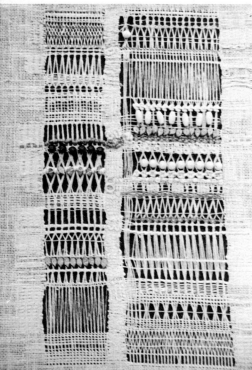

(b)

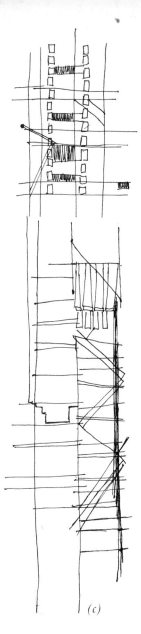

(c)

42–5 Exercises in drawn thread and drawn fabric techniques

42a Used traditionally, and experimentally to create free transparent pattern

42b Work maintains a vertical feeling, with decorative additions of beads, seed, etc.

42c Scaffolding sketches provide suggestions for design. See also 67   *Second Year*

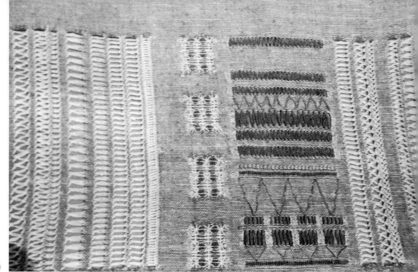

(a)

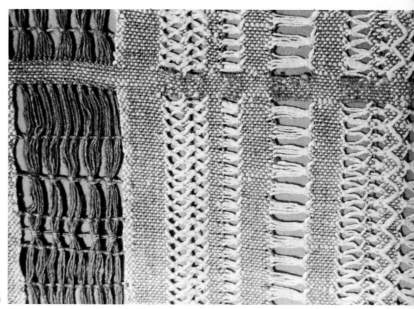

(b)

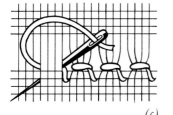

(c)

43a Section of a table-cloth in drawn thread, making use
of linen with dark yellow warp and white weft to increase
the effectiveness of the technique   Elise Curr, Third Year

43b Detail

43c Hemstitch

44a Detail of table-cloth in drawn fabric. Nubby linen
scrim pulled with dark brown linen and gold knitting yarn
Margaret Allan, Third Year

44b Four-sided stitch

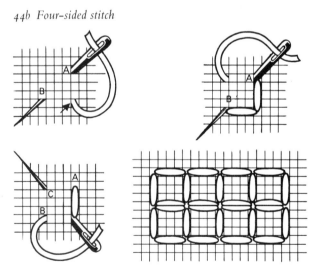

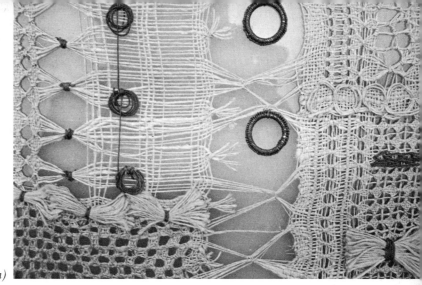

(a)

(b)

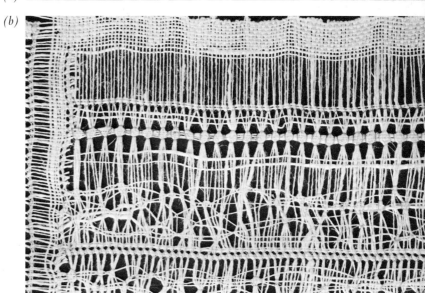

45a Section of a transparent panel, mounted on coloured
perspex

45b Detail of 42a

45c Sketch ideas from various sources   Second Year

(c)

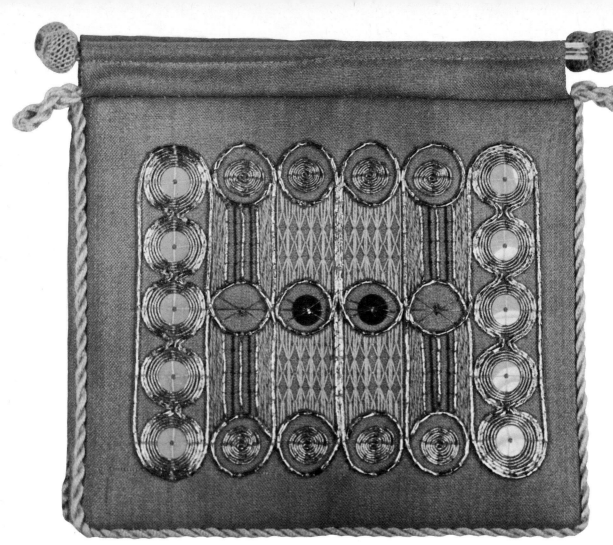

46 *Laying Japanese gold. First piece of work. Design evolved from the idea of keeping a continuous line. See text, also 94, 95, 119b and 173. Photograph: courtesy Embroiderers' Guild*   *Anne Hunter, Third Year*

47 *Museum drawing of a brooch. Suggests affinity between jewellery and gold embroidery*

                    Joan Jeffrey, Post Diploma

GOLD WORK, with its beautiful Japanese gold thread, seems to be the ultimate, the aristocrat of techniques, associated with the highest uses of embroidery in Church and State. It seems far removed from the beginner, but even here, when we look at the initial stages of the technique, we find opportunities for invention. Gold thread is costly, and presents some difficulty when being taken through background material, so the most economical and practical way of using it is to keep it moving on the surface of the work with as few beginnings and endings as possible (*46*). The usual practice is to couch it in place with a waxed silk thread, and since these couching stitches make small noticeable depressions on the surface of the gold thread, it is necessary to space them with great care. Handling gold, then, involves a dual inventive challenge—firstly, the ingenious use of a continuous line design, keeping the thread travelling, doubling back on itself, making not only line formations but also smooth directional fillings with a lovely play of light and shade on their surfaces; secondly, the organisation of the couching stitches into effective repetitions and patterns. Laying gold is a skill which repays careful apprenticeship, for in this technique more than any other, sheer excellence of craftsmanship imparts a bloom to the work (*94, 95*, also *119b* and *173* in silver).

Opportunity in techniques

Neat workers—attempt a gradual freeing of technique through changing scale and texture of yarns (*21a*), and using unfamiliar materials. Try working rhythmically rather than precisely (*34*).

Free workers—discover the fascination of various types of canvas-work, and evolve patterns for floor rugs and chair-seats, using unusual types of yarn and any stitches that fit into canvas (*36–39*).

TRADITIONAL TECHNIQUES
A list of authoritative textbooks on these techniques is found at the end of the book. As indicated in the text above, try to separate the basic ideas behind each technique from the accepted traditional and familiar usage.

Work samplers to investigate the methods and possibilities of special techniques. Try to evolve simple variants in design through the ways of working.

Drawing

Drawing is fundamental to art of all kinds; where there is graphic content this is self-evident. In certain types of work it is not so apparent, but it is there nevertheless as an underlying, implicit quality.

Drawing can take many forms. It can consist in making marks on a surface—pencil on paper is usually the first image to present itself (*48*), but threads on material can also be envisaged. The term can also be used to imply any manner of creating a line or delineating a shape, as by tearing paper (*52a*), or cutting material, or making diagrams. Each branch of art could instance its own special ways of 'drawing'.

Drawing, in the conventional sense with pencil, pen, or brush, may be used simply as eye-to-hand recording, or personal notation, to set down an appearance or impression (*51*). It can be employed to make a likeness, or investigate the qualities of objects or materials, as in analytical drawing (*63a*). Again, it can be a means of expression with an emotional content, and it is certainly a method of communication—a way of describing or telling.

The result, the actual drawing, has a presence, an identity of its own. It says different things to different people. An artist may fill sketch-books with rapid jottings, which are for him merely an extension of his visual memory; other people, seeing the sketches objectively, may find them full of an intrinsic worth, but it is not possible for them to share the artist's memory beyond the appearance of the drawings. Conversely, a teacher may find in a student's drawing more possibilities than the student is aware of.

Drawing should be simple and direct, avoiding stylistic embellishments and preconceived ideas as to what the subject should look like, or how others have portrayed it. Even an approach which feels itself to be honestly inexpert can produce surprisingly useful and personal results. The refreshment of seeing cannot be overrated. To draw a lily, for instance, from memory may produce a symbolic statement of a lily—and this may be what is required; but to look at a lily while drawing it, will make that statement personal, and eliminate the danger of cliché.

Drawing provides direct contact with life, and a well-filled sketch-book creates confidence in any designer. The more one looks, the better one draws, and the more one sees, finding methods of approach within the actual subject-matter. Drawing can be supreme among the arts, but it is also the servant of all forms of design activity.

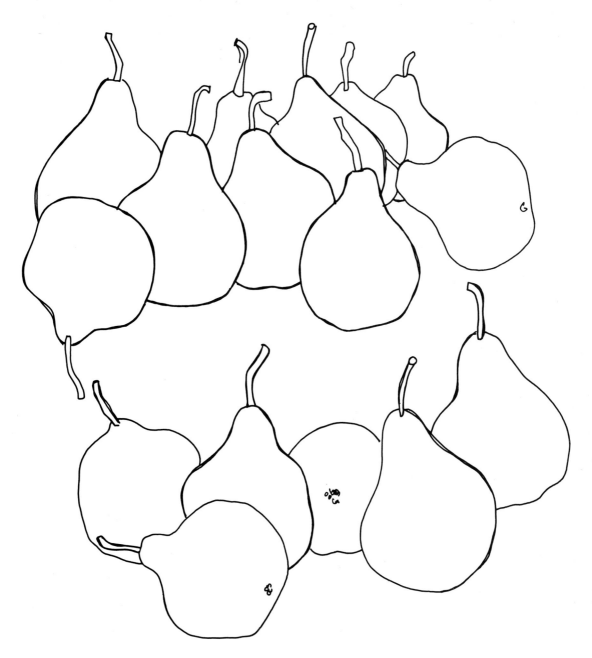

48 Pears, *drawn with pencil on paper: a spontaneous arrangement, looking at one pear from various angles. (Panel from this drawing—see 94)*

Linda Huck, Fourth Year

49 *Life drawing. Suggestion of decorative composition*
Joan Jeffrey, Post Diploma

50 *Imaginative drawing. Creating a design*
Kirsty Davidson, Fourth Year

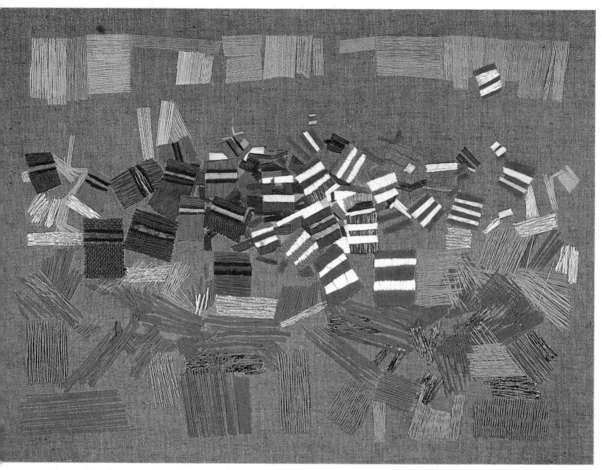

Plate 2 Rugby Match, *50″ × 33″. Design typifies pattern in action. Worked on heavy linen in a variety of yarns, mainly in straight stitches and surface darning*
Anna McCann, Post Diploma

51 Museum sketch-book drawing. Collecting design material. See also 47

(a)

(b)

(c)

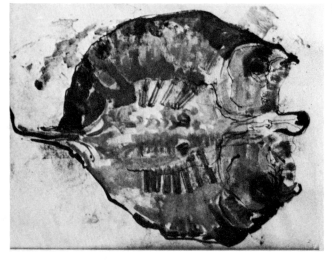

52a Fuchsias, *torn tissue paper and paint*

52b Flowers, *ink and water-colour*

52c Kipper, *paint and pen line*

53 Various media: paint, felt pen, tissue pa
and gum, fine pen and ink, embroidery thread

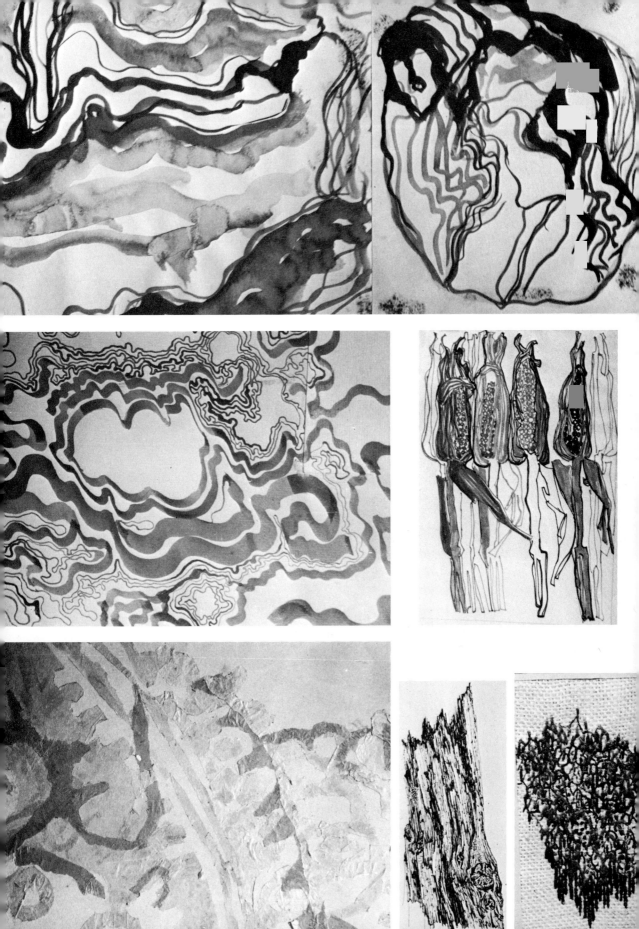

54 The Sun, *impression in threads*
Anna McCann, Third Year

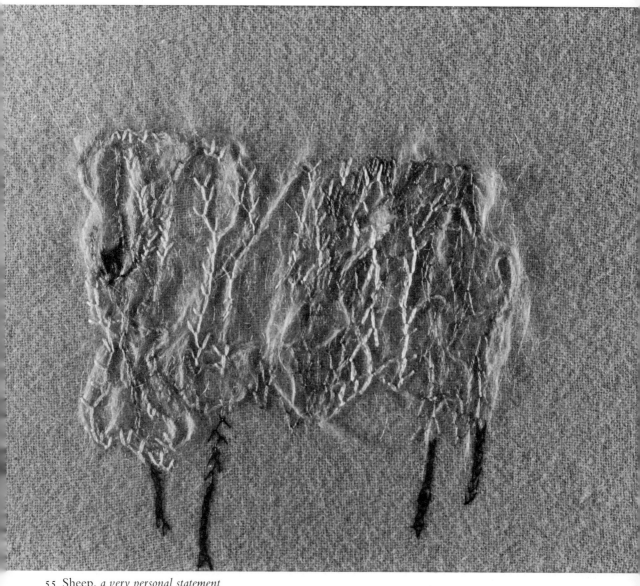

55 Sheep, *a very personal statement*
Jan Machesney, *Third Year*

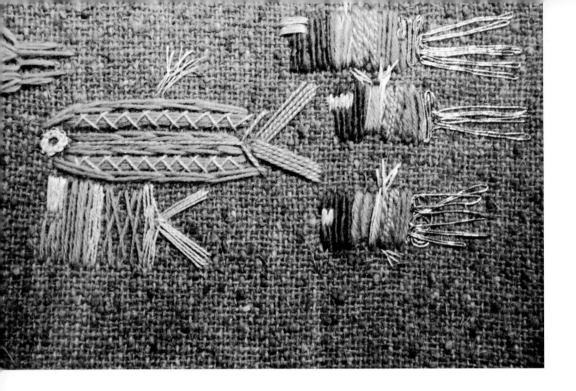

56a *Two details from Fish panel. Woollen hopsack ground, and variety of threads, including gold. Shows very purposeful stitchery, i.e. good drawing*

Elise Curr, Fourth Year

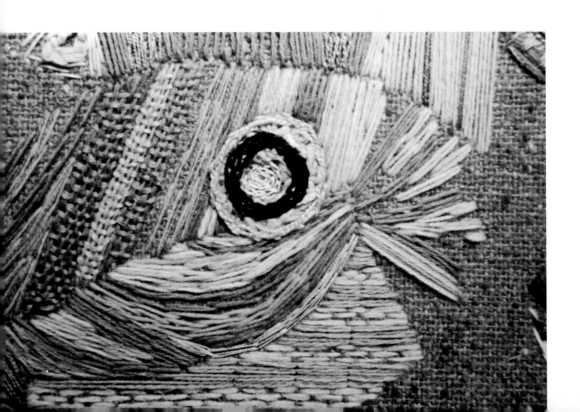

In embroidery, threads have been referred to as line, and stitchery as a drawing medium. By way of illustration, we can compare two details from a *Fish* panel with the stitch extract below (*56a, b*). All three examples exhibit purposeful, sensitive, and direct use of threads and stitches: in fact, good drawing. That the first two represent fish, and that the third has no apparent subject-matter—it may be simply an abstract use of threads —does not in any way detract from the quality of drawing which the third example displays. Drawing does not need to be representational.

56b Detail. Variation of line through choice of yarns and their use. Again good drawing
> Sara Colquhoun, Fourth Year

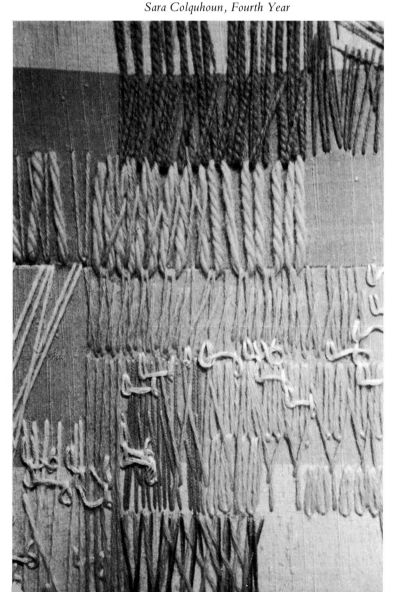

As was mentioned earlier, there is a very close affinity between using threads, as in embroidery, and making marks on paper with pencil, pen, or paint-brush, which is what first springs to mind when the word 'drawing' is mentioned. Two small embroideries of waves, together with the sketches from which they were derived (57, 58) make this clear. The drawings were made by the sea, and the embroideries done shortly afterwards, spontaneous stitchery conveying in each case, more vividly than the original sketch, a personal statement of 'wave'. It is a very lively exercise to work directly from nature to embroidery in two clear steps, making a design statement in drawing, then continuing the thought and crystallising it in embroidery.

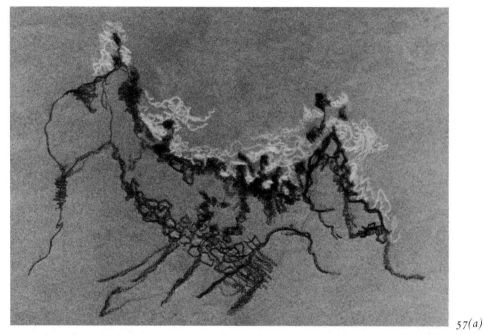

57(a)
57(b)

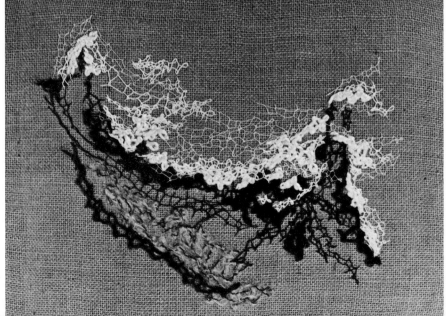

◀ 57a *Sketch of a wave*

◀ 57b *Embroidery from the sketch, 9″ × 6″. Choice of stitch
and thread contribute to drawing*
                    Mairi McPhail, Third Year

58 *Similar exercise to 57*
                    Margaret McLellan, Third Year

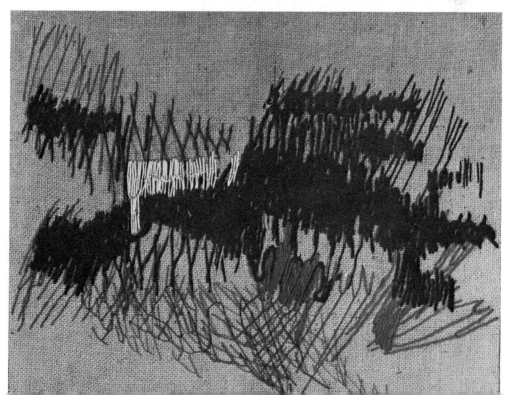

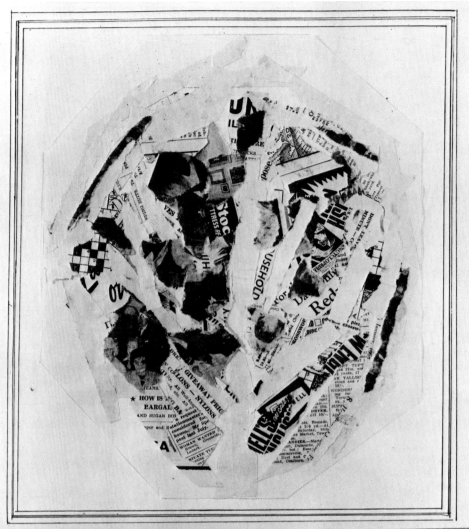

59(a)   59(b)

74

59–62 Cabbage, *drawing, design, and embroidery. Photo-graphs: courtesy Embroiderers' Guild*

59a *Pen sketch*

59b *Beginning to design with newspaper*

60a *Using gum as a resist, paint, and wrong end of paint brush*

60b *Torn tissue paper and paint*

60(a)

60(b)

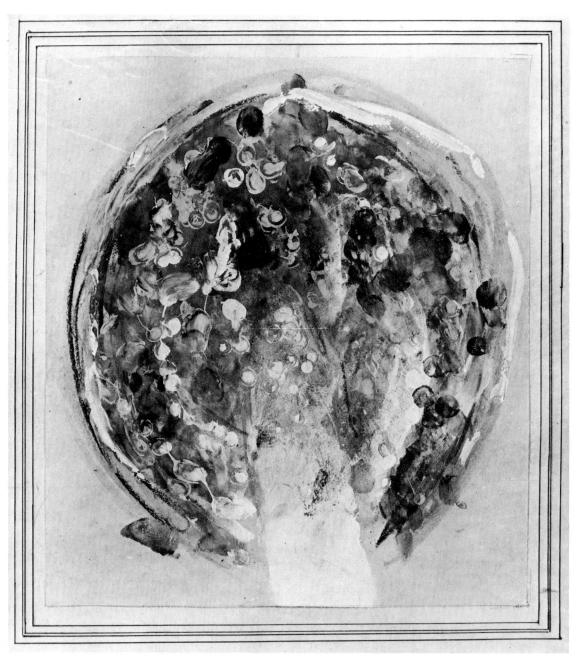

61 *Final design. Shape very simple. Interesting textural effects in paint suggest stitchery*

62 Cabbage, *embroidered on yellow-grey furnishing fabric in black, greys, yellows, and white. Result derives from original drawing as well as from experiments*

Sheila Bruce, First Year

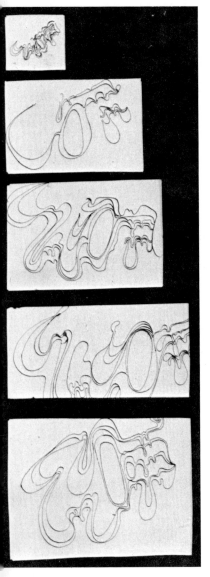

Designers engaged in different crafts develop different kinds of drawing. An embroiderer may use crayons and paints in thread-like movements (*64a*), but it would be wrong to think that this is a conscious attempt to draw like stitches: it is a parallel activity to embroidery. Drawing has an immediate quality. To someone like an embroiderer, working in a slow medium, it can be very invigorating, and at the same time a relaxation. Its rapid and direct treatment of subject-matter can impart vitality and new ideas to the use of threads.

A designer becomes very conscious of the positive quality of his drawing, which can act as a bridge to the next stage of his work (in the 'wave' exercise it formed a direct step to embroidery), or can lead to an intermediate step, sometimes many steps, in the process of creating more formal design (*59–62*). In this case he will assess his drawings, not as representations of things seen, but as source material for design—in other words, as assemblages of marks on paper which suggest lines, shapes, and formations that can be used in many ways (*163b*). Analytical drawing serves this purpose: it is a kind of descriptive search to find simplified structure, from which the designer learns to discard inessentials and create new forms (*116*).

Good drawing is a stage in design preparation, for, as a designer draws he becomes increasingly aware of selection from the subject before him, and also of his arrangement on the page. Drawing gradually becomes instinctive design.

63a Analytical drawing to discover design within a shell

63b Embroidery from drawings, on black linen in shades of ▶
lime green, using rosette chain, twisted chain, and vandyke
variations   *Elizabeth Coghill, First Year*

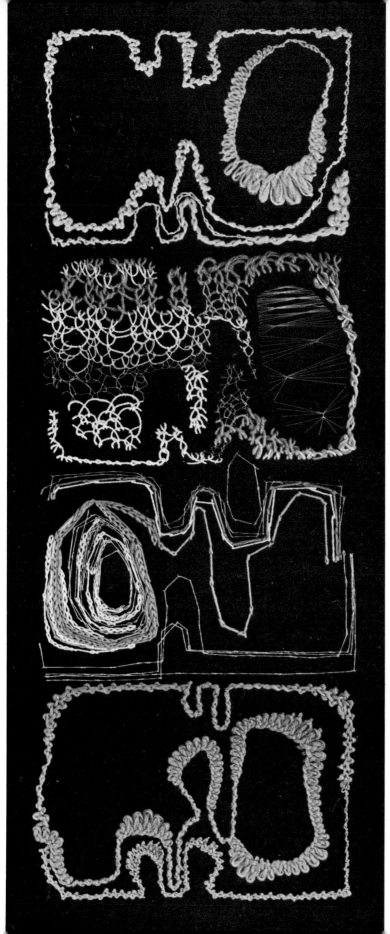

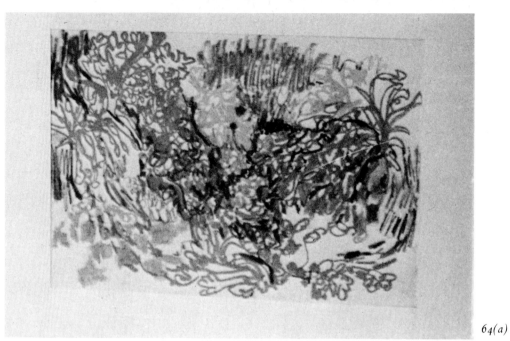

◄ *64a* Seaweed on Rocks, *wax crayon drawing in orange and pink*

◄ *64b* Embroidery from drawing. *White woollen material, wools and fine silks in brilliant shades of orange and pink*
Joan Jeffrey, Post Diploma

65a Freesia, *brush and paint drawing*

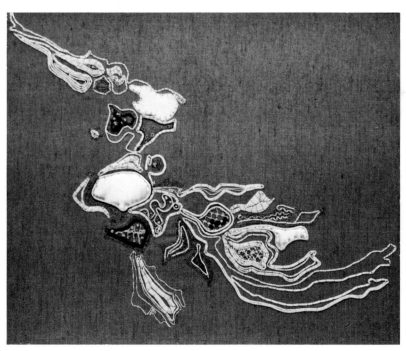

65b Design suggested by drawing. *Silver embroidery on dull green* Catriona Leslie, Fourth Year

◀ *66a Worked directly from looking at the plant: drawing, design, and embroidery crystallised into one activity. Yellow linen background, with various embroidery threads in shades from yellow to green-blue and purple*

Hannah Frew, Fourth Year

66b Detail

Opportunity in drawing

Dispel all ideas of an inability to draw. Regard drawing as something necessary and useful, like writing.

Acquire a modest selection of drawing papers, pens, felt pens, pencils, and crayons, and experiment with them to discover their qualities. These are drawing tools.

Draw different kinds of lines, to acquire fluency and enjoyment in handling the media.

Draw simple things which attract you: house plants, kitchen utensils, sliced vegetables and fruits, soap-bubbles in the sink. Nothing is too ordinary.

Draw for the sake of drawing—to discover. Do not try to make finished pictures, and do not worry if the drawing does not much resemble the original. Do not consciously connect what you are doing with embroidery, and do not ape anyone else's style—that way lies cliché.

EXERCISE   Drawing into embroidery
Keep your drawings and review them. If you find one which even remotely suggests stitchery, use it as a starting-point. Work a small piece of embroidery, looking at the drawing from time to time, but mainly considering the work. This is in no sense a slavish copy, but a stitch idea evolving from your drawing. The result will be quite different from the original.

Gradually your eye will discover what you consider to be embroiderable subjects: those which seem to have a quality of threads and stitches. Making sketches of these will be part of the process of creating an embroidery in this way.

Design

Design is man's expression of life's forces—contrast and harmony, rhythm and balance. Daily living provides elemental and inescapable contrasts, polarities, of which everyone must be aware—

day and night,
life and death,
labour and rest,
waking and sleeping,
food and famine,
joy and sorrow,
growth and decline;

these and many others typify the idea of contrast, of complete antithesis. The sense of contrast is something very fundamental and familiar, something instinctive to all of us, accounting for many of our actions and reactions to the world around us.

The designer has this intuitive knowledge more acutely than most, but he must also develop full awareness of the power of visual contrast, and apply it in his work, using—

line to shape,
plain to patterned,
large to small,
light to dark,
static to dynamic.

These are extremes which can be expressed graphically, creating impact on the eye, and providing essential elements in design.

While each of these pairs of opposites conveys extreme contrast, they can also be seen as end-points of gradually progressing change. Lines may thicken to become shapes; there are degrees of plain and pattern; light gradually becomes dark; between large and small there are many sizes and quantities. This thought conjures up the possibility of vast fields of variation to be explored. Between opposite poles one can visualise a great variety of step by step progressions, an infinity of subtle change. Between black and white there are endless shades of grey. Closely related groups of greys are said to be in harmony; they blend together; they are in accord. Harmony is another element in design.

Dynamic and static, movement and stillness; movement creates change, and rhythm is its path of travel. There are many different kinds of movement —growth thrusting from the soil, wind sweeping over the land, water easing itself sluggishly or surging in waves, flames darting, smoke wafting upwards, man-made machines performing their endless routines, an athlete running with perfect bodily control. Movement like sound is ephemeral; it can be glimpsed, and felt, and conveyed. The designer uses lines to describe his impression of movement, and aims at the ideal of rhythm—a feeling of controlled movement—in his work. The quality of stillness is best understood after motion, and contrasting means must be found to convey it, creating a balance between movement and non-movement. Rhythm and balance are two further elements in design.

The following quotation from a designer's notebook illustrates perfectly the importance of contrast and balance:

'I have often tried to analyse, for my own edification, and so that I can pass it on to students, what it is in today's designs—the best of them—that gives one a tremendous feeling of excitement. I have come to the conclusion that often it is a feeling of tension—the razor balance, typified by the tight-rope walker. No-one would give a second glance at someone walking along a rope lying on the ground, but up there above our heads he progresses along a rope, at this moment in balance, but in one second may crash to the ground. In a good design, one catches a frozen moment of equilibrium; one movement more and the balance may be lost.

'The creation of this feeling in a design, I believe, depends on contrast. One or more of the following must be present to generate this feeling—
    contrast of one shape to another,
    contrast of one scale to another,
    contrast of line to mass,
    contrast of flat to texture or pattern,
    contrast of colour to colour, and tone to tone.
I am sure there must be others.'[*]

To express these fundamental qualities of contrast and harmony, rhythm and balance, man must make use of tools and materials. In all creative work design begins in an understanding use of materials. The craftsman must learn to understand their disciplines, to think in their terms,

[*] Daphne Davidson, *Personal Communication*.

86

and gradually come to use the opportunities for design which they afford. Woodworkers must first discover the properties of wood, silversmiths learn to make basic units in metal, potters get the feeling of clay. In this investigation, embroidery workers have so far had the opportunity to use threads in great variety, and are now designing with stitches—letting the design grow naturally from the formation of the stitches—an intuitive process, referred to earlier as 'organic design'.

Even those who possess a good design sense now begin to realise that something more is necessary than this type of design which grows under the fingers. They feel an urgent need to know more about design itself, its origins, its principles and practices.

DESIGN
initially depends on
LOOKING
training the eye to
SEE
to absorb appearances
to be alert and sensitive in
RECOGNISING
the *elements* of design
CONTRAST—HARMONY
RHYTHM—BALANCE
in
LINE—SHAPE—PATTERN
in order to
CHOOSE
and
ORGANISE
for a purpose

Perception

Seeing as a designer

At night, street lights receding into the distance create strange formations. They appear to be caught up in loops like necklaces, or spread out like constellations. Seldom do they march off in straight lines as anyone with even a limited knowledge of perspective might expect. Reason tells us that the road is dipping and rising and curving, but all evidence of this is blotted out by darkness. Only the lights, constantly changing, remain—selected, isolated, and easily seen. This typifies very simply a designer's vision—the ability, in looking at life, to select and appreciate things for their actual appearance, quite unconnected with use or associations (69), to regard as beautiful the strange contortions of a rusty old bicycle making shadows in a puddle of dirty water, or to find stacks of trolleys in a supermarket a fascinating essay in repetition. Reason, and knowledge of perspective can actually be a hindrance in one's ability to see patterns of lights in the darkness, but more particularly they may get in the way when it comes to recognising the elements of design—*line* as a particular entity, *shape* as area of tone or colour, and *pattern* as natural or man-made formation. To enjoy this simplified kind of vision requires practice and concentration—looking and seeing.

Opportunities are everywhere. In the day-time street buildings provide static pattern, and constantly changing erections of scaffolding and girders, surrounding spires or domes, or heralding new towers, create an aerial geometry. It is not necessary to remember much about geometry to enjoy these lace-like structures (67), nor to speculate on eye-levels before capturing and retaining for future use a design idea of interlacing lines, suggesting interlacing threads (42, 45, 70–72).

Environment, personal interest, and inclination determine the kind of things which 'catch the eye'. Nature is an enormous storehouse of visual imagery, and has always provided inspiration for the designer, each age preferring a different aspect. The Elizabethan embroiderers loved flower heads, the Jacobean designers used large exotic leaves, while slender wafting stems are one of the characteristic features of Art Nouveau. Each generation brings its own new vision to observe how each plant grows in an entirely different and individual way.

People see very differently, and consequently draw from different points of view. Of three artists drawing a field of black and white cows, one, with a knowledge of animal anatomy, is concerned to construct individual life-like cows; another, seeing the cows as animal shapes, might depict them by drawing, as it were, 'a line round each cow'; the third, less conscious of cows, but visually alert, sees them grouped in slowly shifting masses of black and white pattern against a green field.

All the while, subtly, almost subconsciously, the mind of the trained craftsman, as he sees, simplifies, and selects, is working towards an interpretation in his own medium.

Opportunity through fresh vision

Take time to look at:

    your own environment—contrasting places;
    industrial excitement—the country;
    new towns—old villages;
    ordinary domestic articles—things seen in museums.

Change your eye-level frequently.

Look inside things—be inquisitive.

Look at the spaces between things.

Exercise your eye on a train journey:

    station—roofs, signals, cables;
    humanity—porters with barrows, men with cases, women with children;
    glimpses in passing—moving landscape, changing shapes of fields.

67 Buildings surrounded by scaffolding present wonderful opportunities for observing line, geometric shape, and pattern formation. Students' sketches show that even small sketch-book notations suffice to capture design ideas. See also 70–72 and 42c. Photographs: Joan Jeffrey. Sketches: Dorothy Johnston

91

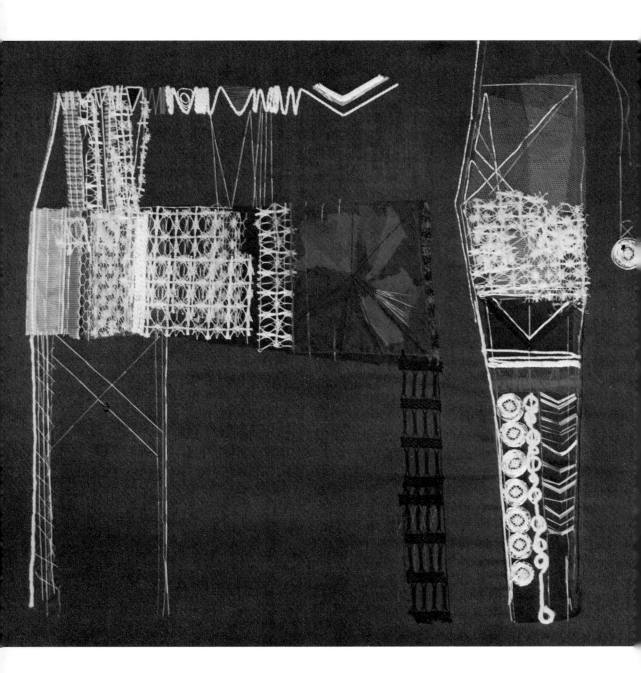

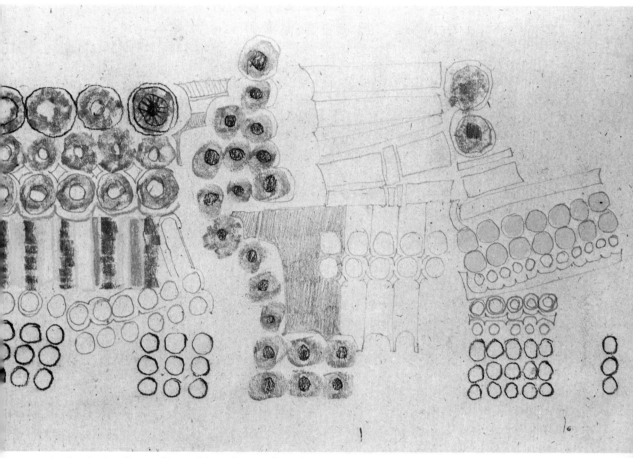

69 Inspiration from ordinary things. Design from drain-pipes　　　　　　　　　　　　　　　　*Hannah Frew*

◀ 68 Docks, *36″ × 25″. Design inspired by cranes. Dark blue background, with overlaid nets, silver in laid work and fine line. Rich colour in the centre. Photograph: courtesy Scottish Design Centre*

Janet Boyd, Fourth Year

93

Line

Line is a means of drawing (*48, 53*). Line is an element in design (*70*). Linear quality has already been observed in the rigid lines of scaffolding (*67*), and the pliant lines of plant stems. A designer must be conscious of line and the effect it is creating, both in actual life and when using it in drawing.

Imagine lines drawn on a page. Vertical lines have, for obvious reasons, what is known as an architectural quality: they stand up, and convey stability. Horizontal lines on a page suggest flatness, calm, ground, and of course horizon. Lines have direction and lead the eye upwards, downwards, to the right, left, or diagonally, depending on how they are placed on the page (*72a, b*). When lines converge in a sharp angled point or arrowhead, they create a very forceful feeling of direction (*81*). If one line is cut by another at right angles, it creates a stop in the feeling of movement—a focal point; the eye rests there. Hence, crosses are used as road signs, and in flags and badges, to attract attention. The Union Jack, for instance, has three crosses superimposed; logically one would expect this triple attraction to create a more powerful impact than the St George's Cross or either of the other two alone. Does it? This is something to solve by looking. Could it be that simplicity is the answer, and that the crosses are cancelling each other out to some extent (*38*)?

To place a spot at or near the end of a line, as in dotting the letter *i*, creates direction and a pause. Any type of spot on its own attracts attention. The eye cannot flow along a line which is constantly being crossed or intercepted. This could be one reason why barbed-wire looks so unpleasant.

Now, everyone knows these simple things, and in the case of road signs acts upon their injunctions, but perhaps they do not appreciate that these are pieces of visual language which enable designers to express what they want to say. They are part of the means of designing. Posters need to have powerful and simple impact; their primary function is to attract attention. Often the designer's method of achieving this is interestingly obvious—by his use of simple and telling line formations. In a much more subtle manner a painter employs the same device. Lines within the painting move, meet, and cross; the eye travels with them round the composition.

Lines and spots are sufficient subject-matter for endless designing. Straight lines have a direct quality; curving and wavy lines are more devious. Paul Klee talked of 'taking a line for a walk', a delightful exploratory

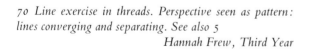

*70 Line exercise in threads. Perspective seen as pattern:
lines converging and separating. See also 5*
                              Hannah Frew, Third Year

71 Contrast of line to shape. Sketch from scaffolding
                              Cathy McConnell, Second Year

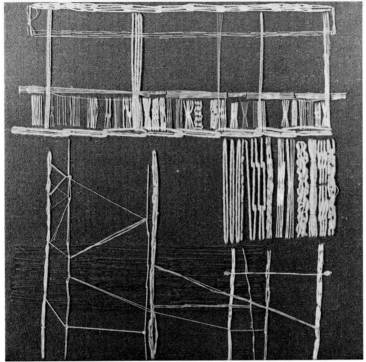

72a

concept. Imagine it travelling all over the page, rushing to one corner, doubling back on itself to investigate other areas, dawdling slightly, zig-zagging about, and finally coming to rest. Think of fresh tyre marks in the snow, how fascinating they are, particularly their parallel quality—two lines travelling together and never meeting. Recall also footsteps in snow, making a dotted line; a dotted line seems to require a little imagination to help it along (*81, 119a*).

Circular line systems exert a particular fascination. Consider a wheel—the spokes radiate from the centre to the circumference. The eye is attracted to the centre by the concentration of lines, but tends to travel to the outer rim and back again. In a bull's-eye, concentric circles growing smaller lead the eye directly to the spot in the centre, but the most powerfully attractive force is the spiral, where the eye has no option but to follow the line round and round to the centre. 'Op Art' designers have used these effects dramatically.

Lines convey movement—precise geometrical movement, or pliant natural movement. Rhythmical forces in nature can be expressed in lines—flowing water, waves (*103*), fire—the necessary repetition of line accentuating the feeling of movement and fluidity. If lines are descriptive of elemental things like water and fire, they can surely be used also to convey abstract emotion—tranquillity, energy, joy (*Plate 5*). Line is a powerful instrument.

The worker will have become much more aware of 'line' in general, and will re-examine her collections of threads, strings, and fibres with a new appreciation of their varied qualities of 'textile line'. Other things of a linear nature—wires, wooden spills, canes, grasses, etc., can bring further variety and begin to suggest ways of experiment. With all these materials for manipulative design, as well as many drawing techniques at her command, she has ample means for creating in line.

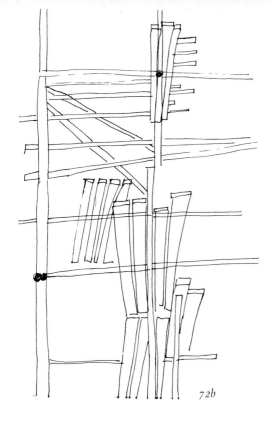

72b

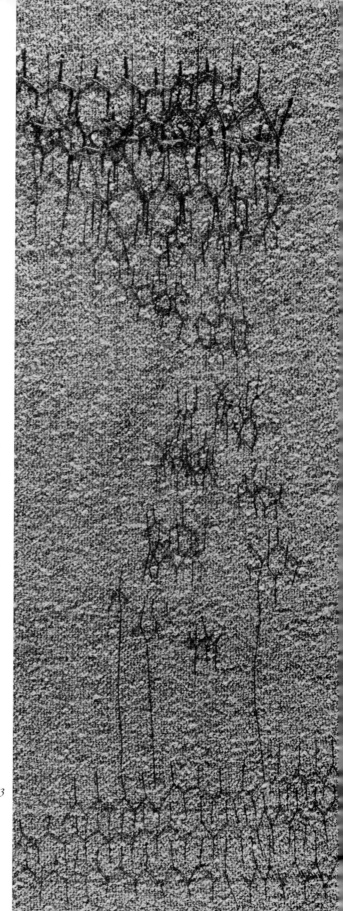

72a *Contrasting quality of line. Various white yarns on light blue in simple stitches*

Daphne Fitzgerald, Third Year

72b *Contrast of vertical and horizontal lines*

Edith McNeil, Second Year

73 Rain, *imaginative one-stitch line embroidery.*
See also 19

Jan Machesney, Third Year

73

74 *Nets have a linear quality: a variety of rhythms and spots*

75 *Ropes make heavy lines, with interesting contrast in fine diagonal line pattern of twists. Photographs: Linda Huck*

76 Wave, *40″ × 26″. Lines convey movement. Bold textural embroidery in carpet yarn, hand-spun wool, and heavy nylon, on a cotton-rayon furnishing twill, in black, white, olive green, and acid yellow*
Catriona Leslie, Fourth Year

77 Fine decorative stitchery based on natural growth design of wood *First Year*

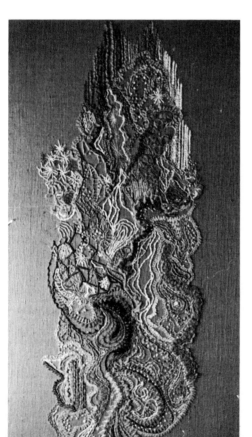

78 Cushion. *Broad bands of stitchery pattern follow rhythmical curves* *Margaret McLellan, Third Year*

79 Explosion, *pulpit fall inspired by the remark, 'Easter is an explosion.' Shows the arresting strength of a cross—two lines crossing at right angles, also its feeling of stability in the centre of an erupting circle. On a pure white silk ground, the circle of satin is surrounded by an intricate mesh of gold and silver with scraps of shisha glass. The design develops outwards, using laid gold, kid, and smooth split stitch in green-gold silks. The cross of laid gold was prepared separately and then applied*

Anne Hunter, for St Giles Cathedral, Edinburgh

Opportunity in line

Line has quality and purpose.

COLLECT
—linear things: grasses, plant stems, wires, etc.
Play with them.

ON PAPER
—use various media: pencils, crayons, inks, and paints, with pens, brushes, and fingers (53), to draw descriptive lines, remembering *harmony* and *contrast*:
    straight—curving;
    powerful—tentative;
    swift—slow;
    darting—trailing.
Do these line effects suggest threads?

ON PAPER OR CLOTH
—investigate the idea of direction. Lines which go:
    up and down;
    out and in;
    crossings and stops;
    diagonally and round.

ON A FRAME (old picture-frame will do)
—with or without a cloth background, create with strings or threads:
    a grid;
    a maze;
    a whirlpool.

ON CLOTH
—with threads and appropriate stitches, do spontaneous line effects from:
    a bundle of barbed-wire;
    grasses;
    rain;
    fences and railings;
    station roof;
    your own ideas.

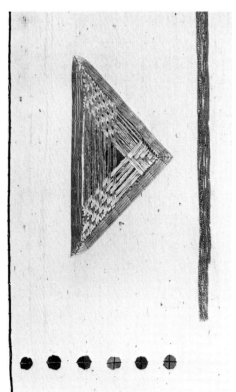

80 Lines join to become shapes
Mairi McPhail, Third Year

81 Triangle gives direction; solid line creates a barrier; dotted line a gentle stop

Shape

Where there are lines, there must be spaces between them. Where lines join up, space is enclosed and shapes are formed (80). If a box of matches is spilt on a card-table, many small white lines will appear scattered about on a green background. If the eye observes the background instead of concentrating on the matches, it is seen to be a complicated ill-defined area of green showing between all the matches; it lacks organisation. But, if three matches are placed together to form a triangle, this is a definite shape, and it isolates a triangular piece of green table from all the surrounding muddle. Four matches make a square, and any number of straight-sided shapes can be defined by the matches. If pieces of white paper are cut exactly to fit the enclosed areas and placed within them, then the shapes are immediately and completely obvious against the green background. The important thing is to be able to recognise shapes. In this instance they are all straight-sided or geometric shapes—triangles, squares, oblongs, diamonds, and so on. People usually have no difficulty in recognising these as shapes, because they do not represent other things; they are just what they appear—geometric shapes.

Squares and circles are regular shapes. They present the ideal of perfection in shape, and also of simplicity, which is a vital element in design. They are statements which the eye assimilates easily, and since they are in complete contrast to each other, they have from time immemorial been used as basic design units. Each possesses a very definite character of its own—squareness and circularity, and these qualities can be accentuated further by individual treatments (by putting squares within squares, for example (82)); or they can be disguised to some extent by breaking the area unsympathetically. If a circle is divided into vertical bands, for instance, the effect is much the same as if it were scored by lines to cancel it out. If the lines radiate from its centre (this is of course natural to the circle) it appears like a wheel. Descriptions of four very differently designed circles appear with the photographs (88–91). When their proportions are changed, squares and circles become oblongs and ovals (82). These new shapes have a feeling of length, of linear direction, whereas the square appears completely static, and the circle suggests radiation or rhythmic movement. These and all other basic geometric figures can be divided and subdivided, both regularly and irregularly, to create an endless supply of varied shapes which serve as units of design. They are ideal for direct manipulative exercises in paper or fabrics.

82 Relationship of basic shapes: squares to squares, circles to squares. Squares become oblongs; circles become ellipses

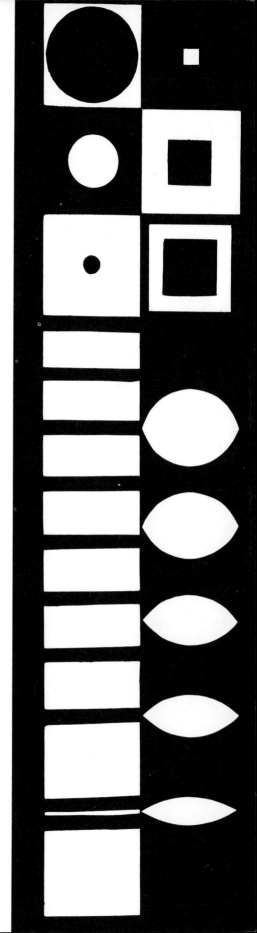

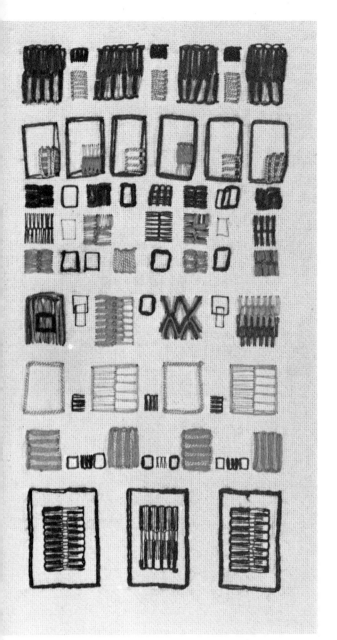

83 Repeating shapes. Sampler using stitches appropriate to squares and rectangles

Margaret McLellan, Third Year

84 Sampler in fly stitch. Variation on triangles and diamonds

Phyllis Campbell, Third Year

85 Sampler using up-and-down buttonhole and spider's
web, to explore the possibilities of circles
                    Ilene McEwan, Third Year

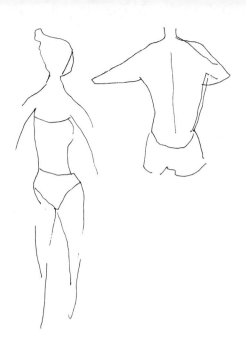

86 *Natural shapes: shells in wonderful variety of shape, and people* . . .

107

Leaving geometry, we observe the world. We look at the country and everything which grows; we look at cities and all that man has made; and we recognise things by their shapes. Recognising is the designer's first act. She recognises a leaf; she wishes to use a leaf in design; she draws the leaf, or cuts it out of paper. Now she has the *shape of the leaf*, a representation of it. It is not the leaf, but a new thing, obtained by looking and cutting: it is a shape. There is little difficulty in recognising a leaf as a shape, since it is flat, but a pear has quite a different quality. It has volume, and is delightful to handle. Something of this delight must be conveyed in drawing it in outline to capture its shape (*48*). In its own way it conveys the same standard of perfection as the circle, but with the added interest of nature's cunning variation.

We could pause here to consider 'variation on a shape', which is a very usual design idea, and capable of producing most interesting results when properly understood. It is obvious that half a dozen oranges are more varied in shape than the same number of tennis-balls, but in addition to variation as between shape and shape, nature shows a rhythm running through the common theme. This can be seen in a beautifully packed box of pears, or in a handful of pea-pods. The theme is pear-shape (*94*), or pod-shape, or whatever motif is being used. If, however, when designing in this way, variations in shape are carried to the point of distortion, the rhythm of the outlines may be lost and the whole effect appear awkward and disjointed.

To return to the use of observed shapes—a bird, used in design, is not a bird, but a shape derived from looking at a bird. It will need to be considerably simplified to make it suitable for the medium being employed. If the bird-shape is made of tweed, for instance, it will be very simple in outline, for the action of cutting it out of thick material will force this, but if it has been well observed and cut, it will be able to convey the essential quality of 'bird' more clearly than might a detailed drawing (*92, 93*).

As with birds, so with animals and people. Those who have, through long practice, developed a designer's type of vision, tend to see people as shapes (*86*)—not in precise detail, as in the past art of the silhouette, but as forms, with their own individuality of mood and action implicit in their outlines. People on park benches appear as sitting shapes, queues are full of standing shapes, and squares are peopled by pigeon-feeding shapes. Groups of people create units (*95*), and people plus things (men carrying ladders and boys with bicycles) make most interesting compound shapes. Women with children show harmonious relationships of form. The familiarity of our own immediate environment and the personalities of people known to us can hinder seeing in this objective way. It is easier in a foreign country, where people are part of a new experience, wear different clothes, and are strange to us: it may, in fact, be their unaccustomed outlines which attract our greater visual attention and create an imprint on the memory.

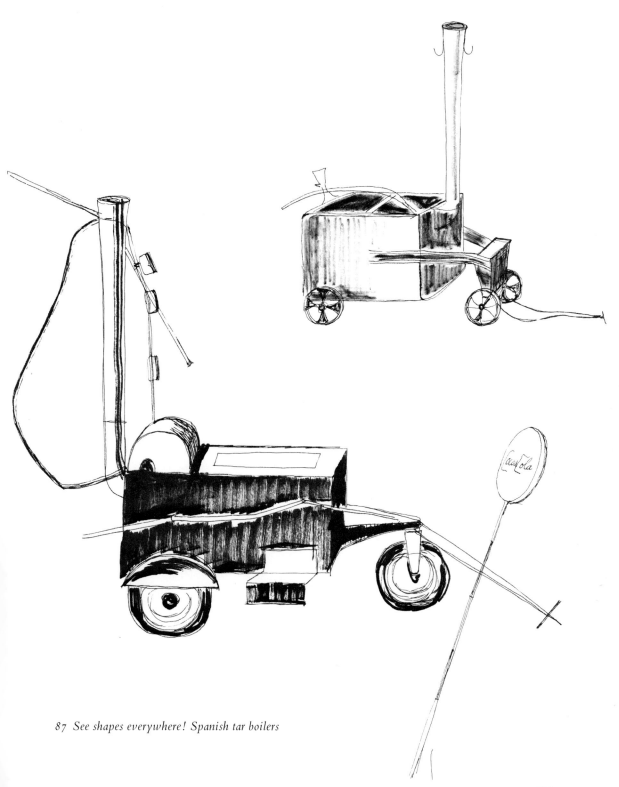

87 *See shapes everywhere! Spanish tar boilers*

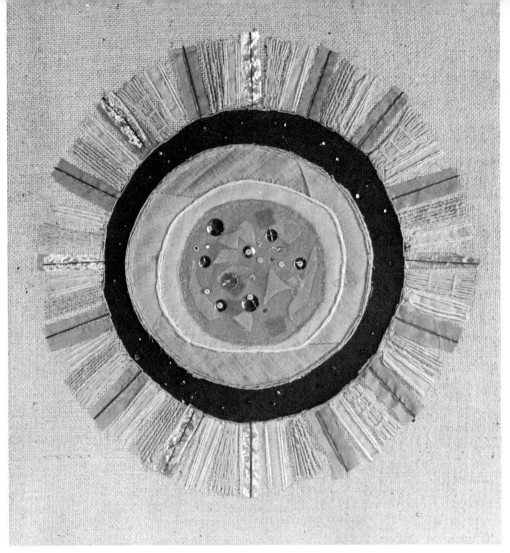

88

88–91 *Four different treatments of the sun*

89   90

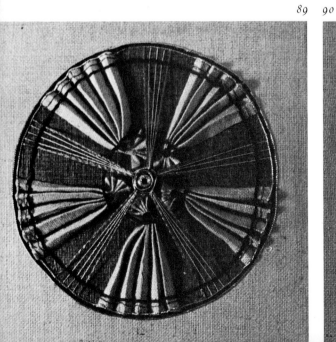

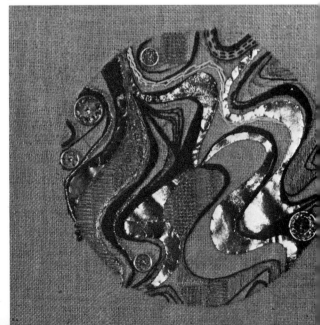

88 Dazzling Sun. *This circle is treated very naturally, and is the most 'circular' of the four examples. On natural hessian, using red, pink, and maroon cottons, with gold raffene, threads, and sequins*   *Christine, aged twelve*

89 Sun. *Pleated fan-shapes of hessian alternate with groups of gold braid radii, and lead to a raised centre. Design has forceful inward thrust and gently rotating movement in the middle*   *Margaret Allan, Third Year*

90 Sun. *Rhythmical design treats this circle sympathetically, but not according to a geometric plan as in (88) and (89). The circle is less a shape in its own right than a container for the design within it. Hessian, with black felt and gold leather, areas of drawn fabric stitchery in gold, and metal rings*
      Kirsty Davidson, Third Year

91 The Sun by Day. *Rich and well-controlled treatment holds the circle together as a dazzling entity, carefully placed within a rectangle. On gold Chinese silk, small facets of variously toned and textured gold materials, leathers, and sequins create a play of light. The rays cast shadows as they rise to meet the frame. (Property of Mr Robin Philipson, R.S.A., R.S.W.)*   *Anne Hunter*

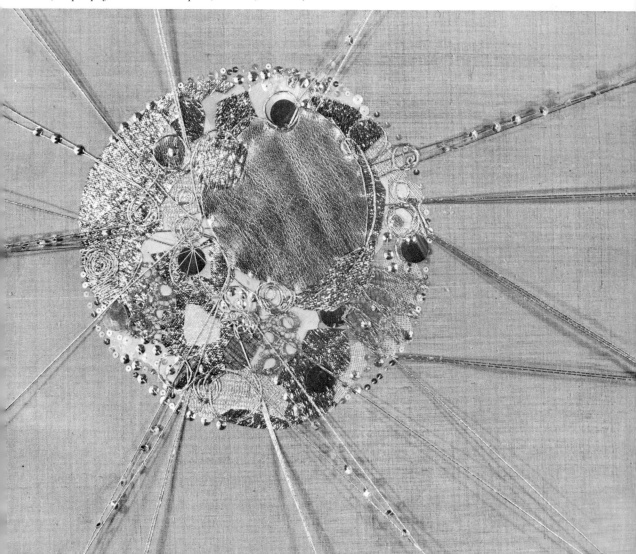

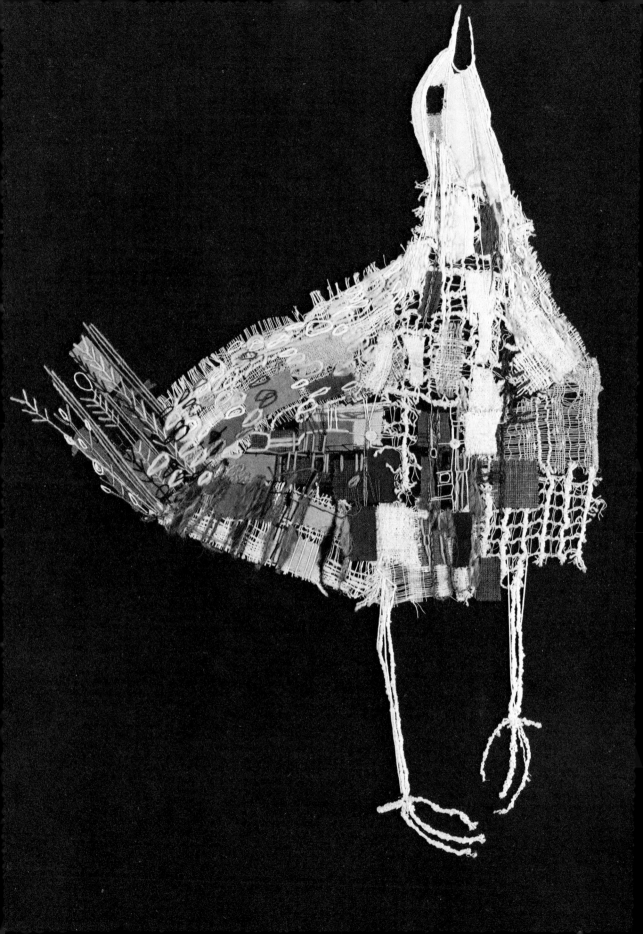

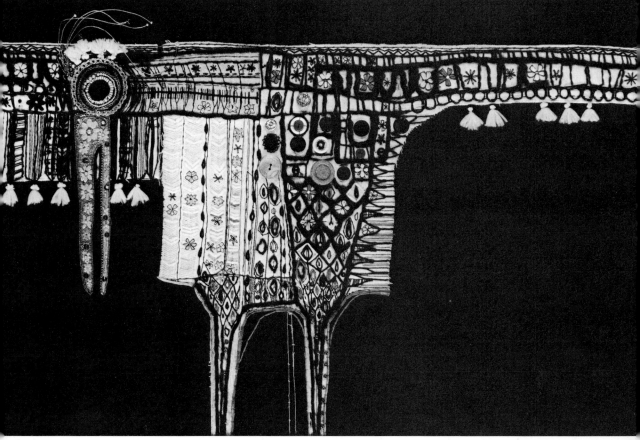

92 and 93 Two Bird *panels by the same artist present very contrasting designs and treatments. Quality of design does not depend on nearness to nature at the one end of the scale, nor on abstraction at the other, but on whether the treatment is good of its kind and consistent within the work*

92 Seagull, 24″ × 30″. Sensitive simple shape, created in a fabrication of nets, linens, and stitches. There is good balance of interest between the bird-shape and technique employed. (Purchased by Mr Arthur Liberty) Pat Ross

93 Spanish Bird, 36″ × 24″. Much more abstract in design, this provides a good example of what is known as 'positive and negative form'. The strong simple bird-shape cuts the area completely making the positive statement; the resulting black areas are the negative form; all are necessary for the complete design within the rectangle. (See 'Composition'.) Feathers are freely suggested by the embroidery worked in areas of graded intensity, delicate and pale on the breast, heavy pattern on the wings and leg, using buttons and circles for further emphasis. The eye is a circle of gold with pearls, and the beak is composed of pink flowers. (Purchased by the late Anne Redpath, O.B.E., A.R.A., R.S.A.) Pat Ross

95 Gold People, 14″ × 10″. People as units of design. Technique and 'symbolic figures' well matched. (See page 117.) Background of dull gold silk, with gold kid and laid work. Photograph: courtesy Embroiderers' Guild.

Fiona MacCallum, Fourth Year

◀ 94 Gold Pears, 11″ × 14″. Pear-shape used as a motif and repeated with variations creates a rhythmical line. (See page 108.) Worked in simple gold technique, with padding and kid, the pears lie on a background of orange and yellow chiffon, with gold net at the top. A development of the drawing of pears (48)   *Linda Huck, Fourth Year*

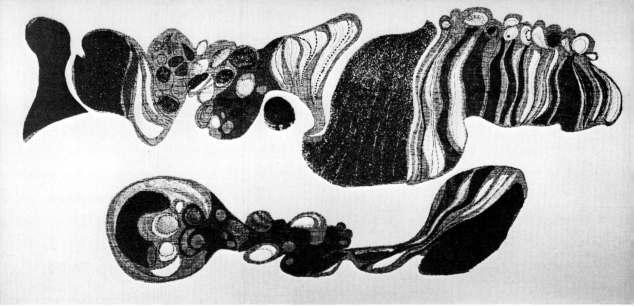

96 Trees, 52" × 21". Design based on drawing of a group of trees, abstracted and, unlike Pears, taken far from its point of origin to form a composition of two agreeably contrasting shapes. Black materials of varying density: tarlatan, nylon, and vilene, with gold lamé, on a white ground, with fine line stitchery

Jan Machesney, Fourth Year

97a Painted design derived from a 'daffodil' drawing: very formal. Embroidery almost entirely in chain stitch, using crimson, scarlet, purple, and bright yellow wools on a dull gold background   Mairi McPhail, Third Year

(a)

97b Very stylised design from cabbage leaf. Lines of varied density used as space filling. Bottle-green to turquoise-blue wools and linens on white woollen material

Magdalen Carnegie, Third Year

There are many ways of drawing the human figure, and its use in design is a very personal matter. Children draw people unselfconsciously, and with great success. Their figures are mainly symbolic (*108*). The designer is seeking her own symbol through observation and intuition (*179*, *184*). The American artist, Ben Shan, was highly gifted in his portrayal of ordinary people. His drawing depicts humanity, with economy of shape and inevitability of design.

A designer not only recognises but assimilates shape. She takes it for her own. She can change it to suit any particular purpose she has in mind. She may become fascinated by the shape itself, quite apart from what it originally represented (*96*). She can change it by exaggerating some aspect, as in a caricature. She can distort it to make it look taller, or squatter, or more elegant, or comical, or for any other reason she has in mind, but there is a kind of meaningless distortion which says nothing personal, a type of gimmickry, which should be avoided. She can make several versions of her shape, using it wholly, or in part, dividing and rebuilding, until finally she is satisfied with a new shape which she has abstracted from the first version (*97*).

When shapes are used together, in pairs or in larger groupings, their association is controlled by observing their similarities and differences. They can be used to create harmonious relationships, or effect sudden contrasts.

Making shapes in embroidery

Any kind of shape can be created in embroidery stitchery. The whole aspect of space filling has such wide possibilities for invention in the use of threads and stitches that any attempted directive must prove inadequate. It could be useful, however, to look back to 'Stitches', to recall elementary methods, and relate these when possible to other examples later in the book. It was shown that individual stitches, worked in areas, determine shape (*13*, *18*). Building stitches can make characteristic structures (*19*, *20*), and repetitions of threads and stitches can fill a space to render it flat (*15*, *152*, *and Plate* 7), or follow its contours in a more sympathetic manner, as shown in two very different treatments of a daffodil (*97a*, *135*). Pattern can break up an area (*109*, *93*), and textural effects, rich in stitch variation, make a bold statement (*22b*). Stitchery can create descriptive shapes (*161c*, *162c*), and imaginative renderings of ideas (*164b*); in fact, it can deal with shape in limitless ways.

Fabrics as a subject are considered later in the book, but it is obvious that cutting material provides an immediate way of obtaining areas of colour and texture. Cutting is very important. It is a means of drawing, and a line made with scissors can be as strong and spontaneous as one made by any other method. A confident approach is best. Dispensing with a guiding line, the worker should 'look and cut', keeping the flower petal, or her own sketch or whatever she is using as a model in view. She can then study the result, and change its contours to suit her ideas. While the worker cuts materials to experiment, she begins to discover their suitability for certain kinds of shape in preference to others. Thick fabrics make good simple areas, felt and plastics give clear-cut edges to geometric shapes, while intricate outlines require firmly woven fabrics. In time she develops a sense for this affinity between textural quality and shape. At this stage the most important thing is to regard all shapes with a critical eye. As in every other design activity, creating shapes needs practice, and also ideals. The designer should keep her eyes open, and try to find, particularly in nature, simple satisfying shapes to provide standards.

Opportunity in shape

COLLECT SHAPES
—from nature:
    actual objects—stones, shells, leaves, etc. (*86*). Handle them.
    photographs of birds, fish, fruit, flowers, etc.
    photographs of landscape and natural manifestations (*98–103*), (shapes too large to handle).

CUT FROM STIFF PAPER OR CARD
—basic geometric shapes in various sizes, to make a collection for manipulative experiment (*82*).

CUT AND TEAR FROM TISSUE PAPER
—spontaneously:
    shapes from flowers, fruit, etc.
Examine them and evolve new shapes from them.
Find shapes to abstract in rocks, stones, etc.

DRAW
—leaves and the shapes between them.
—fruits singly and in groups.
—sections of fruits, vegetables, etc.

CUT
—by looking at your drawings, in paper or cloth.
Make rapid sketches of birds, animals, people. (These often contain the
'essence'—the essential simplicity.)
Cut from these, and be critical of the shapes.

MAKE CLASSIFICATIONS OF SHAPES
—simple, regular, irregular, particular, etc.

IN MATERIALS AND THREADS
—work stitch areas with one-stitch, evolving good shapes.
Build shapes with suitable stitches:
    two shapes of the same kind;
    two contrasting shapes.

ON A FIRM MATERIAL BACKGROUND stretched on a frame (*160c*)
—manipulate shapes cut from felt, vilene, plastic, etc., making:
    formal arrangements (*Plate 1*);
    free curving arrangements.
—experiment with circles, breaking them up sympathetically, and in other
ways (*88–91*).
—use squares in the same way.
—fix satisfactory arrangements with simple stitches.

VARIATION ON A SHAPE
Choose a simple shape which appeals to you.
Cut versions of it in paper, and arrange them in groups.
If the group looks 'inevitable' it will be a good arrangement (*130*).

MAKE AN EMBROIDERY
—using shapes of material and stitchery as space fillings.
—carrying out your own ideas.

Pattern

Since the beginning of time man has been learning from nature, taking its formations and adapting them to his use—inventing the wheel; discovering how to measure, and converting nature's geometry into a precise and reliable science; being inspired by an avenue of great arching trees to build a cathedral to the glory of God, with high vaulting and fan-tracery like branches magically turned to stone; using, as Paxton did, a great water-lily leaf to instruct himself in how to build a Crystal Palace. Primitive man, living close to the earth, created art forms to explain the forces of nature to himself, and to appease his gods: modern man, with his highly sophisticated sense of order and his vast technical ability, has used his own mental functions as a model and created the computer for his use. In these illustrations nature is for man a pattern, meaning a model or prototype for his inventions. That is one meaning of the word 'pattern'.

If, however, we say that nature is full of organic pattern (98, 99), this creates a different impression, a feeling of life increasing by addition and repetition, of plants growing and multiplying in an ordered and rhythmical manner. Each species produces a different kind of growth formation, or natural pattern. The earth itself can appear like a giant patchwork. Its strata lie in layers or undulating bands, and its minerals are found in crystalline form. Stems under the microscope show cellular structure, and leaves have an obvious pattern. There are special things, like honeycomb, spiders' webs, cacti, and snowflakes, each with very individual construction (116–119, Plate 7).

Nature clothes birds, fish, animals, and insects in patterns suitable to their habitats: leaf-shapes, spots, lines, and chevrons disguise the jungle creatures, and areas of colour follow the delicate structure of a butterfly's wing. The sea creates moving pattern (103), and its creatures bear the imprint of the waves—shells (86), and weeds, and fish moving in shoals. Flights of birds, and clouds move in pattern, one formation seen against another.

There is pattern at every stage of growth. Trees seen in line against the sky look like parallel columns with arches between them. Their branches make lattice patterns, and the bark appears like protecting scales (98). When the tree is felled, evidence of its age will be seen in a pattern of concentric rings on the section of its trunk, and on closer inspection the cut wood will reveal a cellular pattern, which becomes ever more intricate the more it is enlarged under the microscope.

98–103 *Pattern in nature. Photographs, taken at Culzean, Ayrshire* *Joan Jeffrey*

98a *A frieze of wind-battered trees makes delicate tracery on the sky-line amidst a textural pattern of undergrowth*

98b *Pattern of tree bark*

99 *Pattern from the earth. Rock showing contrasting formations of line and shape*

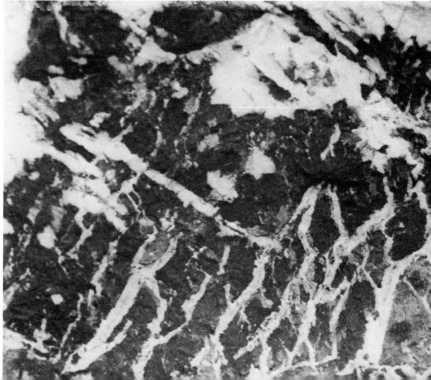

100a Pattern on the sea-shore. Glistening repetition of stones, dotted with small crustaceans and festooned with seaweed

100b Rhythms on the sand

*101a Pattern of distant breakers, shelving rocks, wind-
flected water, and corrugations of sand formed by the tide*

101b Oyster-catchers in formation on the sand

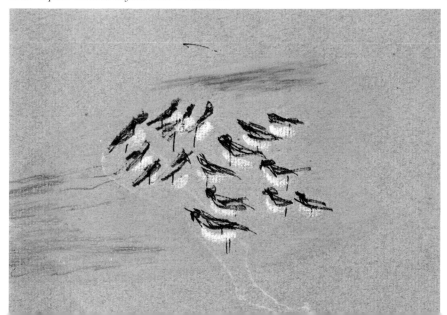

123

102 *Pattern of water-lilies. Smooth areas of oval leaves, with an occasional flower, becomes a jostle of fan-shapes*

The designer can see and express these structures in line and shape, and in fact they provide her with a vast store of source material from which to derive inspiration for her work.

Man reacts to the rhythm of nature. He creates pattern in his actions, not only in building and construction of all kinds, but in his sense of order in living, in organising his work, his home, his food, his leisure. Gardens have pattern—fortuitous, as in an expanse of allotments, or formally planned, like Hampton Court. Games are pattern of action, from Chess and Mah-Jong to Rugby Football (*Plate 2*). Dance is rhythmical pattern of movement. Music is pattern of sound. Newspapers and books are laid out in pattern. Commerce displays and sells by pattern. Life is pervaded by it. Man enjoys pattern; he takes an instinctive pleasure in arranging.

In our investigation into design so far, we have recognised *line* and *shape*; now *pattern is the link-up*, providing methods of *repetition*, systems of putting together, grouping and organising all forms of design units.

Pattern-making begins very simply:

One line adds to another to form stripes.

Lines vary direction and join each other to make battlement and zigzag patterns.

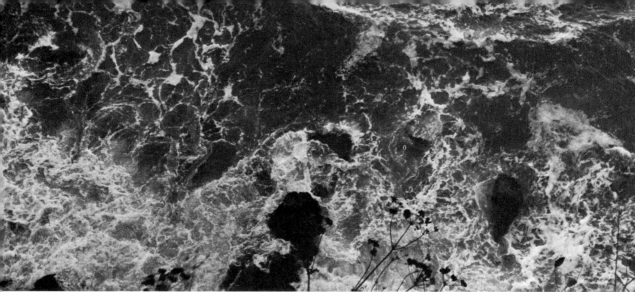

103 *Sea. Wonderful patterns of movement. Foam marbling the underside of a wave, and water surging round submerged rocks*

104 *Drawing of fishing boats at Crail   Hannah Frew*

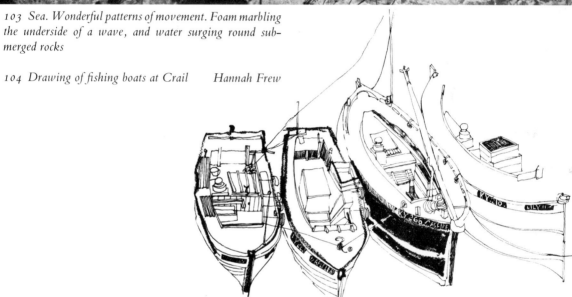

Units repeat in rows, vertical and horizontal, or in alternating arrangements.
Lines cross each other to form square grids, lattice formations, etc. (*70, 126*).
Geometric shapes repeat according to their nature.
Squares form checks, and oblongs can build brickwork pattern (*83*).
Triangles duplicate themselves to make diamonds, which fit together in lattice formation (*84*).
Hexagons make honeycomb pattern, and other shapes repeat according to their kind (*133*).
Circles follow each other like beads on a string; touch, leaving shapes between them; link together in alternate order as in chain-mail.
These few examples of repetition are so common that they form part of a natural usage for putting lines and shapes together, and are basic to pattern design. They are found in collections of historic pattern, which have accumulated from every civilisation. Each one represents a method of pattern-building, not only for simple line and shape arrangements, but also as a foundation for increasingly intricate systems of pattern design.

105a *Pattern at work. Girls threading looms*

105b *Drawing of a dobby*   *Joan Jeffrey*

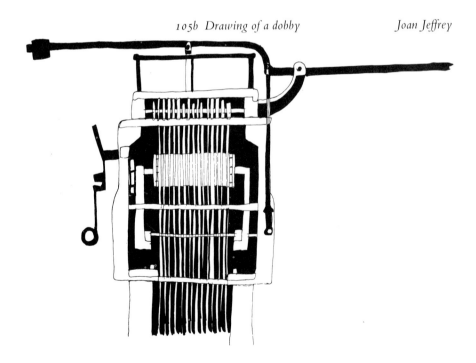

*106 Pattern, planned and accidental. Architecture with
reflections and weathered stonework*

◄ *107 Pattern of children's faces. Very young children used embroidery rings, to help them in sewing down pieces to make a face. Group exercise: arranging the heads*
Kirsty McFarlane, Lecturer,
Craigie College of Education, Ayr

The photographs accompanying this chapter aim to illustrate nature's all-pervading pattern and sense of rhythm, from which the student should constantly seek inspiration. Various 'Sea' and 'Wave' embroideries throughout the book have their origins in this larger concept of pattern. Looking for pattern in nature, however, can begin simply, by studying small things. Concentrated scrutiny of one shell, or of a sea-urchin, can yield useful and personal results. The 'fir-cone' drawing (*116*) demonstrates a search for pattern units and formations, and the rapid notes from a pineapple (*122*) show that drawing need not always be careful and detailed to capture essentials for future reference. Careful looking is all-important. These discoveries from the cone and pineapple could be adapted and used in a manner similar to that indicated in the 'net' exercise (*124*).

Illustration *112* shows three stages in pattern development: (*a*) drawings derived from parts of a shell; (*b*) simple pattern structure built in tissue paper and paint; (*c*) embroidery, using the design as a plan and enriching each part of it with inventive pattern stitchery.

Man-made structures (*67*) embody pattern formations, also contributing ideas to the designer. Architecture can provide window pattern (*127*), arcading (*150*), mosaics, and many other points of departure for pattern design; textile substances such as nets and meshes (*124*, *126*) provide examples of good proportional repetition; an African mask (*115*), and design from nineteenth-century kitchen utensils (*51*) manage to convey a wider view of man's use of pattern.

◄ *108* The Slide. *Play pattern. Group work: making people and arranging them. See also (95) and 'Shape', page 117*
Kirsty McFarlane, Lecturer,
Craigie College of Education, Ayr

Opportunity in pattern

Make a collection of units for pattern-building exercises:
(1) *Line*—strips of paper, straws, matches, etc.
   Spot—adhesive spots and stars, metal rings, and washers.
(2) *Whole geometric shapes*—squares, oblongs, triangles, diamonds, circles, and ovals, each shape in various sizes, cut from card or stiff paper.
(3) *Cut up geometric shapes*
   Squares, cut into smaller squares and triangles.
   Circles, cut into semicircles, quarters, segments, rings, etc.

Using the collections as numbered above—on a firm background of paper or card:
(1) Plan line and spot patterns, and observe the spaces between units.
(2) Plan patterns of:
   squares and oblongs, singly and together.
   triangles and diamonds, singly and together.
   circles and ovals, singly and together.
(3) Reorganise pieces from cut squares, to make decorative squares (*123e*).
   Reorganise circle shapes to form decorative circles (*23, 113*).

Develop your own ideas for pattern-building.

PATTERN FROM NATURE
Collect objects and photographs which show pattern formation.
Make sketches from them, to capture pattern ideas (*122*).
Develop these ideas, by repeating, reorganising, and changing their scale.

FREE PATTERN
—on paper, using crayons or paints, draw and paint freely:
   line patterns;
   ideas from edges of shells;
   ideas from plant stems and tree bark;
   ideas from fish scales and bones;
   your own ideas.

DESIGN FOR EMBROIDERY
—using the method indicated in the description of (*112*) in the text:
   discover a pattern idea, and sketch it;
   plan a design in tissue paper from the sketch for stitchery pattern.

ANALYSE
—patterned papers.
—printed fabrics, etc., to find their types of repetition.

Pattern in embroidery

'Pattern', applied to embroidery, brings to mind a wealth of examples from all parts of the world and all periods of time. It appears like a labyrinth of styles, techniques, and applications, in which it is difficult at first to find direction. Faced with a large subject to investigate, it is best to decide on a relevant area of interest, and ask simple questions. So, let us try to find out from a practical point of view what pattern does. Two answers are useful in this context: pattern decorates, and pattern plans. To illustrate these functions, we can enlarge a little on two examples from very different types of embroidery mentioned already in the 'Historical review'.

Let us look first of all at peasant embroidery. Most people are familiar with some examples of this type of decorative needlework. Used widely on household articles, and in its more elaborate forms as decoration on national costumes for festive occasions, it appears as the very embodiment of pattern. Belonging to particular regions and cultures, varying greatly from place to place, its common characteristic in all areas is a traditional practice of working, in which design and technique have evolved together through many generations. A great deal can be learned from looking at all types of peasant art (51). Its instinctive appeal lies in the obvious nature of its design. It is easy to follow the thought which pieces together one metal facet after another to make a necklace, or even to imagine hands painting the brush strokes of flower and bird motifs on wooden articles. In embroidery, pattern grows from small beginnings. Stitch by stitch, counting the threads on hand-woven material, geometric shapes form naturally, and build gradually into units of design. These can be repeated regularly, alternately, by counterchange, in symmetrical and many other ingenious arrangements, to form borders and areas of rich pattern.

This is, of course, a general description of the basic method, which must be understood to vary from one traditional technique to another, but it puts the emphasis once more on the pattern-forming nature of embroidery stitches, stressed earlier in 'Stitches' and 'Technique', and also on the importance of organic design. The modern embroiderer need not regret the lack of an inherited tradition of working, for, strictly adhered to, it can become a groove; it would seem rather to be an advantage not to have preconceived ideas about how stitches should be used. The lesson comes from the methods employed in peasant design, and from the appeal of its basic simplicity. Stitchery is a storehouse of pattern units for experiment in decoration.

The second illustration, to show pattern as a plan, relates to examples of *Opus Anglicanum*—the Syon Cope and the Butler-Bowden Cope, both of which are in the Victoria and Albert Museum in London. They demonstrate pattern as foundation design. It was very necessary for the designers of these vestments that the large semicircular areas of which they consist should be reduced to shapes of practical size to contain the ecclesiastical figures, which

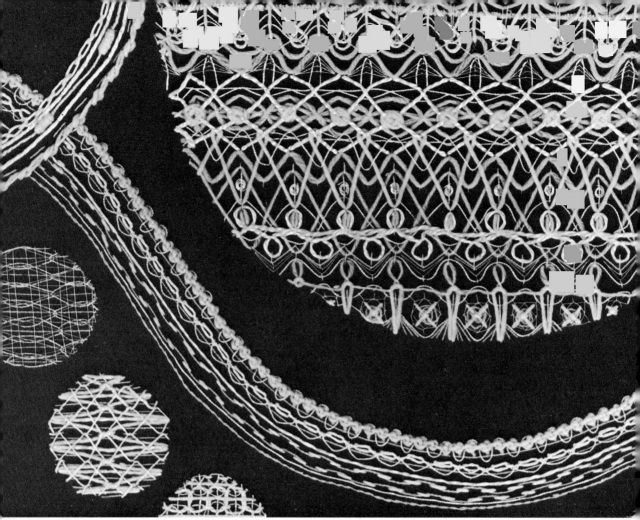

109a and b Two details from (159). Ingenious pattern-building in stitchery, using many kinds of white thread on a black tweed ground. It is interesting to follow a particular thread to discover the stitch being used. Small circles show tonal variation by changing density of stitchery

Marilyn McGregor

form the main theme of the work. The pattern structures employed are in themselves very beautiful, and no less important from the point of view of the design as a whole than the figures. The surface of the Syon Cope is divided by an interlaced structure of geometrically formed links, called 'barbed quatrefoils'. This creates two types of shape, the larger kind enclosing biblical scenes and figures of Apostles, and the smaller, cross-shaped compartments, holding angels. The Butler-Bowden Cope uses a different framing pattern on its dark red velvet background. Very decorative Gothic arcading, worked in gold, creates niches to enshrine the figures. Both arcading and figures are graded in size from large to small as they rise from the lower edge of the cope, creating a pyramidal effect of Gothic arches when the garment is worn. These two examples illustrate pattern used as a large repeating design to break up an area—to plan space. This very usual design device has been employed in varying ways in practically all historical periods when the formal nature of design was prized. The curving stems on the Elizabethan stomacher, already mentioned, were

performing the same function in enclosing flower heads, as were the quatrefoils, but in a natural rather than geometric manner.

The design idea of breaking up an area in whole or in part by pattern structure is very useful to the worker when planning for various techniques. Obvious examples include drawn thread work and drawn fabric, when applied to table-cloths and other articles which need good layout design before the work begins. Patchwork can be planned in this way, as old examples show, and the method has been extensively used in the design of canvas work chair-seats and stool-tops. Because it has been used a great deal, and is a very simple method of planning design, it must not be thought ordinary or dull. If the shapes are of good proportion and arranged imaginatively the result has every chance of being visually exciting.

These two aspects of pattern in embroidery which have been considered —organic stitch design and planned layout—in no way conflict; each prepares for the other. This theme runs through the whole of design in embroidery: the small invention which grows under the fingers and the large concept keep each other in mind, come together, and complement each other.

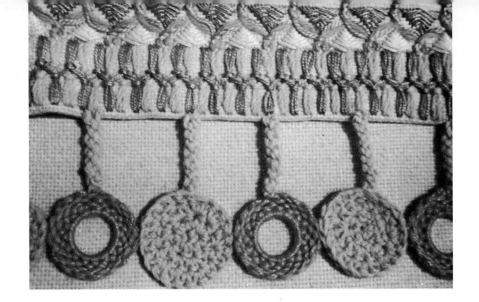

134

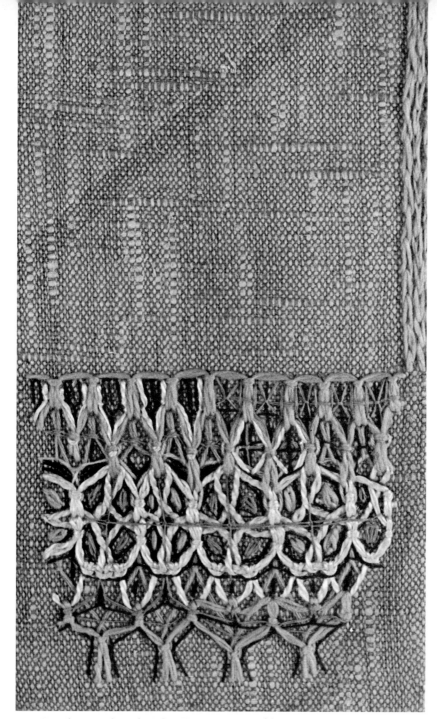

111 *Sampler in reds and pinks. Free repetition of basic stitch, up-and-down buttonhole, worked alternately as in Cretan stitch. See 20*

◄ 110 *Details of stitch patterns on a jerkin. Multicoloured embroidery, using coton perlé and wool on yellow hopsack*
Joan Jeffrey, Fourth Year

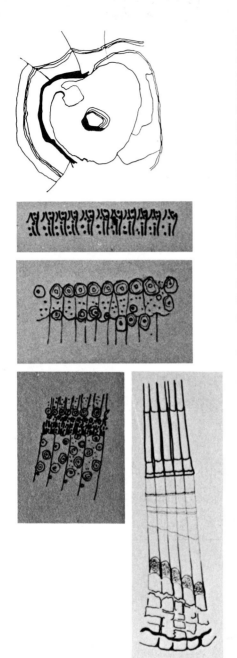

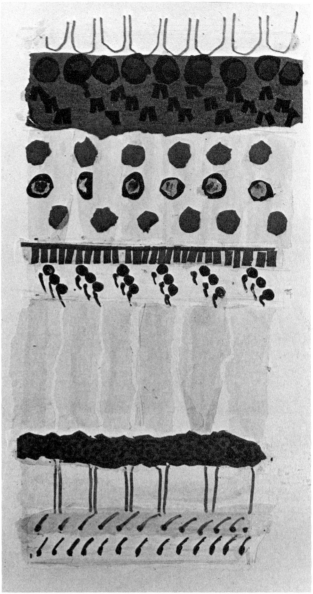

112a Planned pattern. Drawings investigating pattern in shells

112b Pattern design planned in tissue paper and paint from drawing

112c Drawing and design provide ideas for using stitches ▶ in pattern formations. Grey background, turquoise, mauves, blues, and white   First Year

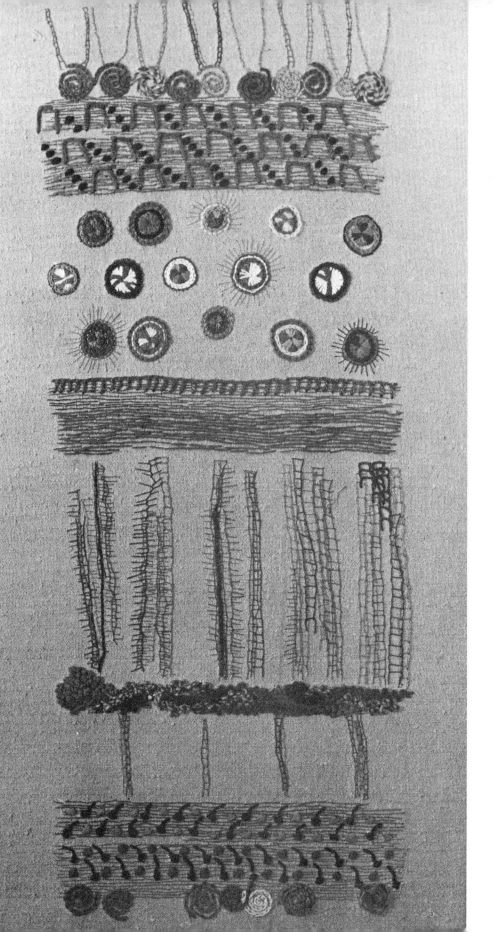

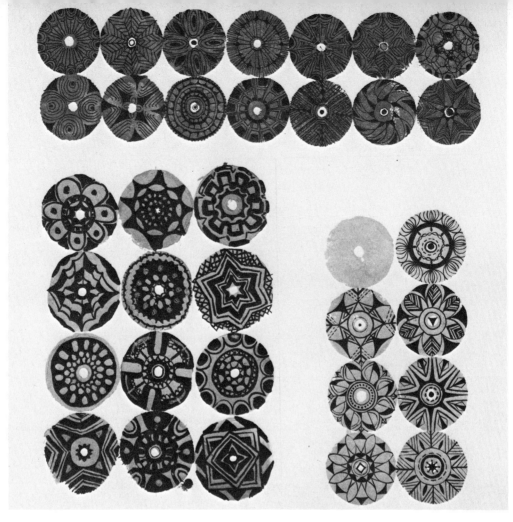

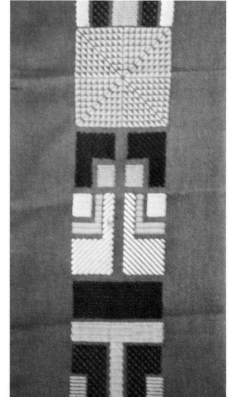

113 *Opportunities to make formal circular stitch patterns. Designs by junior students. See also 23*

114 *Panel of pattern-darning worked down the centre of a table-cloth, in black, white, and yellow on a tan background. Detail shown in 39g*   *Hannah Frew, Third Year*

115 *Drawing of African mask. Example of indigenous pattern for a particular purpose*
                    Joan Jeffrey, Fourth Year

116 *Analytical drawing of a fir-cone, showing its spiralling growth formation and dovetailing units. This drawing is a preparation for selecting and organising, as shown in 124*
                    Linda Huck, Fourth Year

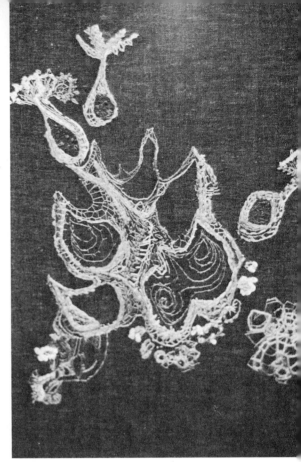

117a and b Nature's cellular pattern. Sea fan, and detail showing affinity to stitchery

118 Cellular quality in stitchery. Detail of 'Cauliflower' embroidery First Year

117b

Illustrations from a thesis on 'Winter in one-stitch Embroidery'

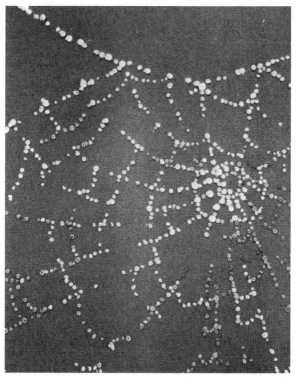

119a Cobweb, *suggested in delicate dotted lines of French knots. Pale colours on soft green*

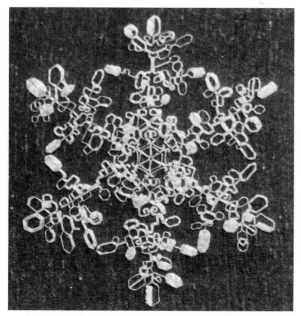

119b Snowflake. *Silver couching in continuous line, on brown silk background. See also 46*

Agnes Hamilton, Fourth Year

120 Rocks, *30″ × 18″. Design based on irregular pattern found in rock formation. Black, white, and silver stitchery panel* Kirsty Davidson, Third Year

121 Landscape pattern. Fabric and stitchery panel in pinks, mauves, scarlet, and soft greens. Design developed by repetition and variation of kindred shapes. Inspired by painting landscape* Fiona McGeachy, Fourth Year

142

Opportunity in embroidery pattern

Keep in mind *contrast*:
   in threads—size, kind, colour, tone.
   in stitches—size, line to shape, etc.

PATTERN FROM STITCHES
Varying your background material, continue to experiment in building pattern directly from stitches, evolving new and more ambitious designs.

Referring to 'Opportunity in pattern', page 130, carry out in stitchery your design based on the idea in (*112*).

PATTERN AS DECORATION
Relate your stitch patterns to larger ideas, such as your free line paintings. Examples: cushion (*78*), borders for jerkin (*110*), circles—various uses (*113*). Try out your own ideas.

PATTERN AS A PLAN—REPETITION
—make use of your geometric pattern ideas:
   to plan a patchwork of straight-sided shapes (*35*, *Plate 1*);
   to plan a canvas-work design for a cushion or stool-top (*36*, *39*), bearing in mind the samplers which you have worked;
   to make layout plans for tray-cloth or tea-cloth in drawn thread or drawn fabric technique (*43*). (Cut newsprint gives a very good impression of areas of open-work.)

CELLULAR PATTERN FROM NATURE
Work small samplers from your sketch ideas (*122*), and also from any of your collected objects which display this quality (*117*).

PATTERN FOR NEW TECHNIQUES
Plan for other types of work (*39g*, *114*), and your own new ideas (*40*).

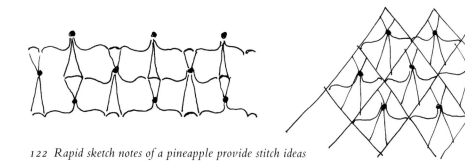

122 Rapid sketch notes of a pineapple provide stitch ideas

Designing

Designing is a conscious action which can be described as *choosing* and *arranging*. Very simply, it can consist in selecting lines and shapes, and arranging them according to a plan and for a special purpose.

Many of life's quite ordinary activities provide excellent instances of this, table-setting being a good example. The table is an area, either square, oblong, circular, or oval. The first action breaks this up into sections by placing mats, and if they are brightly coloured they form a good contrast to the wood. To use instead a striped table-cloth would change the appearance of the table-top, but would not perform the useful function of defining each person's place. Knives, forks, and spoons, with their linear quality, now do this, enclosing areas which acquire an exclusive feeling of one for each person. Plates, which are circular, and perhaps in more than one size and colour, come next. Napkins may be folded into triangles, and glasses and cups introduce the element of height. There is pleasure, not only in arranging these things, but in recognising their separate characteristics, in knowing how they differ from each other, and in choosing them, firstly for their usefulness, but also for their contrasting qualities of line, shape, size, colour and texture.

This teaches us the importance of choice, and leads us on to look more closely at what it means. Choice is an act of discrimination, of taking some things in preference to others because of their appearance and usefulness. It implies personal taste, which is seemingly instinctive, but conditioned usually by background and training. The student of design becomes aware of the fact that constantly exercised choice, selection and rejection of special qualities for special purposes, is a refining process, and that eventually what might be called 'informed choice' becomes second nature. This is the very essence of designing. It suggests sensitivity, a feeling for the quality of materials, and for the use of line and shape; it also suggests an appreciation of affinities and differences.

In any work, 'first choice'—the initial statement—is a brave personal step forward. Even if governed by necessary conditions, it has about it a large element of freedom. For a designer it could be the first brush stroke on paper, the first shape cut, or the first stitch worked. It is the point of departure, the all-important start to the work, on which second and further choices depend. These must then be seen in relation to the first choice, and controlled by the desire for harmonious similarities, or, by contrast, the need to express change and dramatic effect, in each succeeding stage of the work.

The four examples which follow illustrate in some detail choice and organisation in action from the designer's point of view.

Think firstly of physical arrangement, manipulation, the movement of actual selected things. For an exercise, these could be matches, jigsaw pieces, flower petals, shapes cut from paper or material, sequins, straws—anything that seems to provide a supply of useful units—spread out on a board or other background. Even an arbitrary distribution of chosen pieces, got by tossing a handful on the background, provides opportunities for looking at the results, and the ease with which the effects can be changed makes it a very convenient method for beginning to plan designs. There is no rigid convention to be followed here as in table-setting. Planning is experimental, but ideas for arranging can begin from such simple concepts as repetition or variation of a unit, as in *123* and *124*. As we have seen in 'Pattern', both geometry and nature's formations suggest innumerable ideas for organising lines and shapes into design.

The second example concerns a designer working graphically—drawing or painting lines spontaneously on paper. Choice here is governed by an idea, which can be subconscious or the product of reflection and deliberation, influenced by memory or imagination. Choice is always present, determining what his hand performs, however rapid and fortuitous the result seems to be. It involves not only lines and shapes, but where he places them and the resulting spaces between.

Next we can consider an embroiderer starting on an experimental piece of work, one without prior design preparation. She is involved in a whole chain of selections, firstly as to materials and threads, then as to stitches and what she will do with them. Will the technique be controlled or free? Where will she begin on the background? This is a slow process and needs insight throughout. Since it is in no way a mechanical activity, each stitch quite literally needs a thought to itself (*125*).

Lastly, a landscape painter, with no desire to portray the entire panoramic view before him, selects a certain feature from the scene, and, determining its place on his canvas, paints it in as a first act. It may be a strangely shaped field, prominent by its bright colour, which he feels will be the keynote to his whole composition.

The purpose behind all four instances is experiment in design. All involve choice of units or subject-matter, considered placing by some plan however tentative, and at each stage attempted evaluation of the result. How can this evaluation be done? Is there anything to help the eye's instinctive search for balance and interest in arranging? What kind of judgement is involved here? It is again a matter of harmony and contrast, this time particularly in relation to sizes and quantities, and the visual effects which can be created by their variation. This brings us to the subject of proportion.

(a)

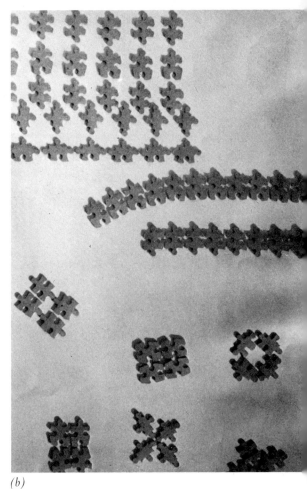

(b)

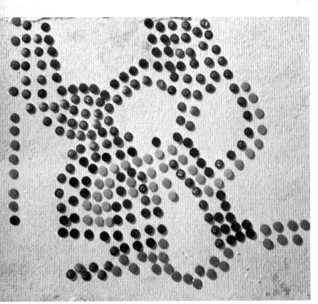

(c)

Manipulative design. 'Choosing and arranging'. Repetition of a unit

123a and b Jigsaw pieces

123c Drawing-pins in a board

123d Felt shapes and stitches

123e Painted geometric shapes

123f Embroidery stitches in square units

(d)

(e)

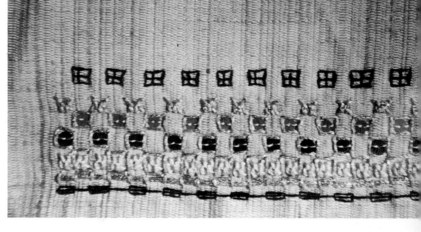

(f)

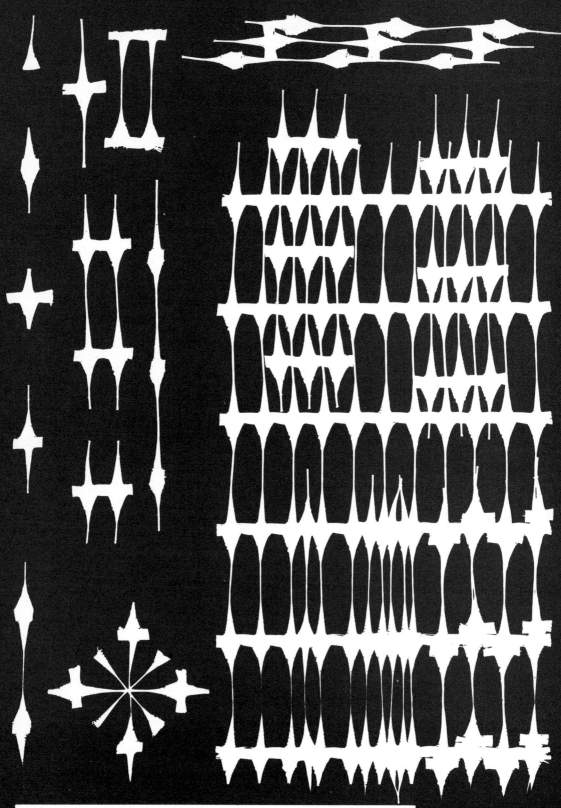

Analysing and pattern building with well chosen net. Net used is proportionally exciting, with its relationships of slender white column to open area and horizontal white bar. (Captions on page 150)

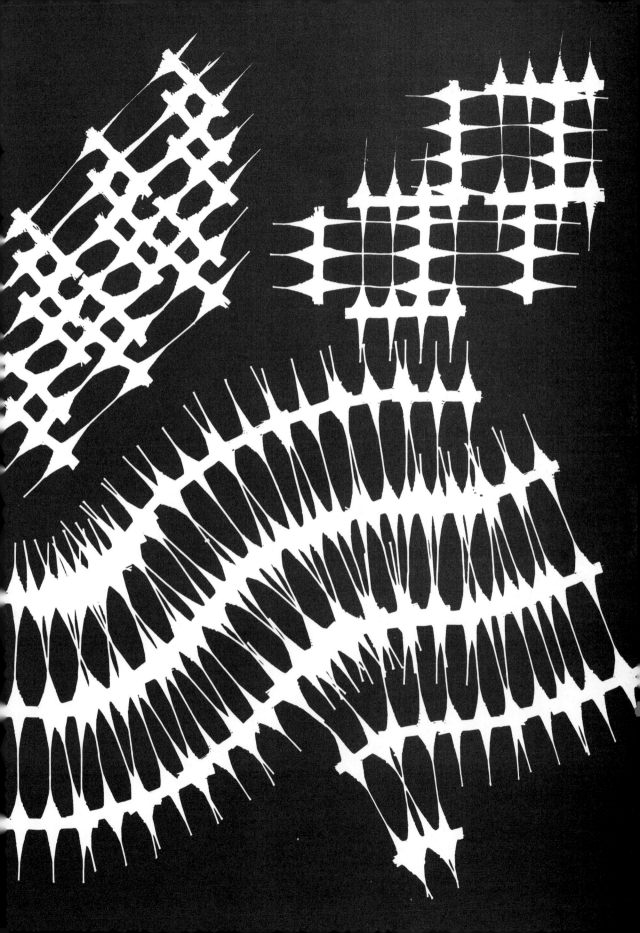

Pages 148–9

124a At the left, analysis produces small units, all of which could be organised in repetitions and combinations to form pattern. In the larger area, pieces of net are superimposed on the original structure to form various new designs, all keeping to the original vertical and horizontal lines of the net

124b Further experiments with the net create diagonal, square, and rhythmical patterns. The intention is to discover methods of designing. The results need not relate only to net, but provide ideas for using threads, stitches, and other materials

125a 'Choosing and organising' with threads and stitches. 24″ × 50″. Design lightly suggested by a row of houses and a path. Embroidery very direct, on a white woollen background with a large variety of woollen yarns, fine thread, sequins, and scraps of gold mesh   Margaret Allan, Third Year

125b Detail

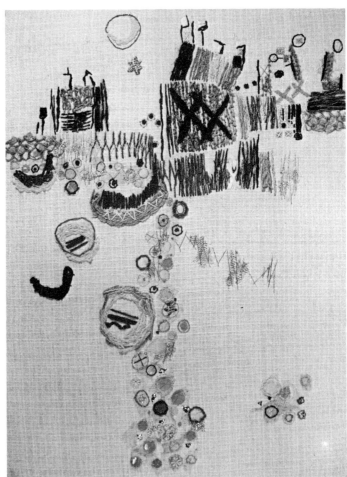

125a

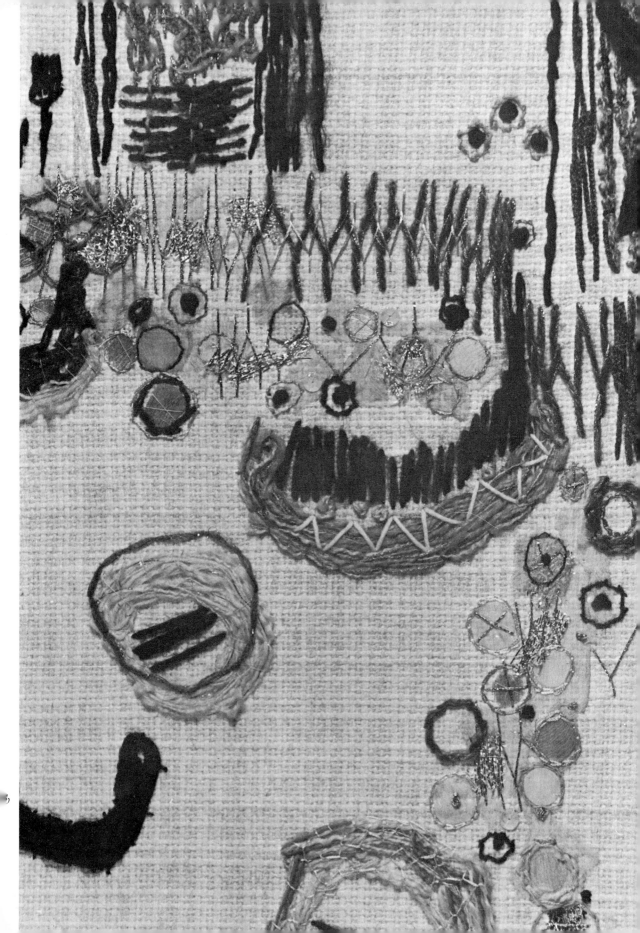

Opportunity in choosing and arranging

CHOICE
Using your collections of stones, shells, flowers, etc., pay great attention to their appearance, and organise them for varied qualities—for *similarity and difference* from the points of view of shape, colour, texture, and so on.

SELECTIVE CHOICE
—conduct a private game. Look at things:
   in the home;
   in shop windows;
   anywhere.
—ask yourself—would I choose that?
   with delight? Why?
   with reservations? Why?
   not at all? Why?

MANIPULATIVE DESIGN
Using the 'net' exercise (*124*) as a basic idea, find other materials—cloth, paper, discarded packaging, etc., which have good possibilities, and experiment with them.

PAINT
—on a good-sized sheet of paper a thoughtful arrangement of well-chosen lines and shapes—spontaneously!

OUTDOOR SKETCHING IN CRAYON
Select from the prospect before you. You are not a camera, and need not 'put everything in'.

CUTTING FABRIC SHAPES
As a development of your sketch, make a panel with materials fixed with unobtrusive stitches.

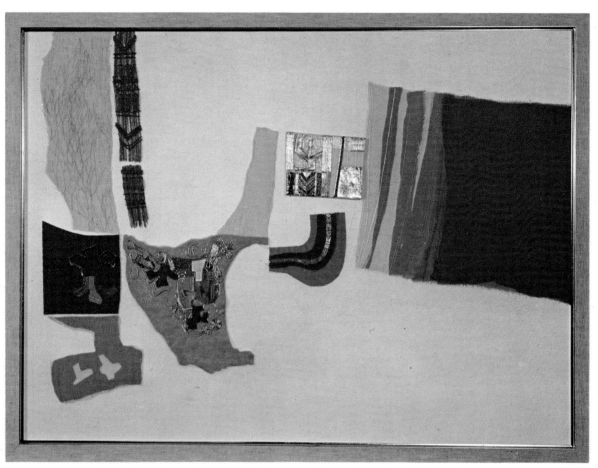

Plate 3 Forms on a White Ground, *43″ × 26″. Composition of dissimilar shapes in contrasting fabric effects and techniques. Layers of chiffon, raised area of formal gold work, free pattern on green felt, counterchange, soft shadow-like stitchery, and surface weaving*　　　　　　　　　　　　　　*Hannah Frew, Fourth Year*

Proportion

Proportion is the name given to the relationship of sizes to each other, and implies the practice of using measurements and quantities in comparison one with another. Where there are two dimensions, height is compared with width, and in solid objects—which have height, width, and depth—all three measurements are considered together.

Proportion is a fundamental element in design. Everything has size. Everything is made up of quantities which can be measured, and which determine shape. On their interrelationship depends, to a great extent, whether an article is distinguished or commonplace in its appearance. Architects and all who are concerned with three-dimensional design work constantly with instruments, measuring exactly. Their work would be impossible without exact calculation. Painters and designers in embroidery do not so obviously rely on exact measurement, but seem to reach their conclusions by exercising aesthetic sensibility. But what is aesthetic sensibility in this context? It is an eye, sensitive and well trained to detect difference between one size and another, to assess the effect of one quantity against another, together with an ability to realise that these relationships are controlling factors in the visual language of design.

Every art student is introduced to the study of proportion by being given various exercises in making stripes, to assess the effects of quantities seen together (*126*). Equal stripes of black and white are found to have a tantalising feeling, each fighting for supremacy, and the smaller the stripes the more dazzling the effect. If black is increased even slightly there is a sense of relief; something is resolved; black has become the background; variety has taken the place of monotony. Black can go on increasing until white is merely an occasional pinstripe—a case of extreme contrast; similarly white could take over and swallow up black. Different permutations of stripes have different effects. There can be gradual developments and sudden breaks. A dark stripe can become light through regular gradations; a band of small even stripes can alternate with a bold contrast; the possibilities are endless. If grey stripes are added to black and white, the problem of organising the stripes become more subtle and interesting, because this introduces an intermediate tone. With the addition of further tones, the possibilities for stripe permutation are increased, and wide complexities of tonal variety become possible. There is danger, however, in over-complication, lest, through lack of precise organisation, a desirable overall simplicity be lost in a mere disorderly mixture of sizes which cancel each other out.

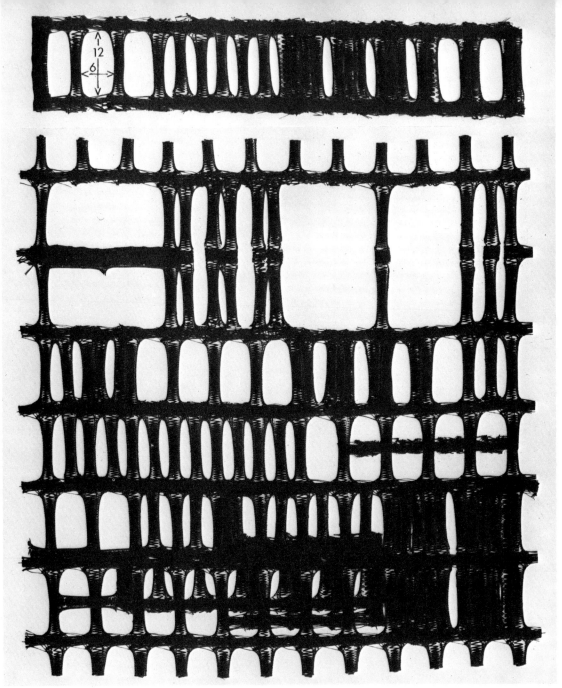

126 *Exercise to illustrate variety in proportion and change in scale, using black oblong-meshed net as a basic structure. The actual size of the rectangular spaces in the net is 12″ × 6″ (see top left), and of the upright black lines 12″ × 2″, measured in tenths of an inch. Starting with this proportion of 6:3:1, by cutting and manipulating the net, the areas of space and lengths and thicknesses of line have been changed to create a variety of new proportions. Change in scale is apparent as white areas decrease in size from top to bottom and black lines correspondingly increase in density. The rounded nature of the net does not allow precise measurement, but such methods of working are useful for experiment, and provide an easy means of observing contrast in size, and the different effects created by the varying relationships of white space to black line*

Excellent subject-matter for the study of proportion is provided by present-day architecture, with its tall blocks of offices and flats which are rising in all our towns and cities. Their construction not only dictates the stark economy of their outlines, but determines their fenestration—these huge areas of contrasting surfaces in which glass predominates (*127a*). Their form and pattern are of such initial simplicity that they rely entirely upon their architect's individual use of proportion for their effects. The design thought, basic to the monumental check patterns of their exteriors is play on a rectangle: dividing and subdividing with vertical and horizontal bands to break the enormous surface into patterns of smaller rectangles (*127a, b*). Some of these buildings succeed in being very dramatic in outline, seeming perhaps too slim for their great height. By this particular contrast, they typify what is known as 'extreme' proportion—a very large variation between dimensions. The opposite to this type of relationship is called 'mean' proportion, where differences between quantities are very slight. This can be used to produce a subtly fascinating effect on the eye, and is a very usual design device to create interest (*130*).

To leave modern building and visit a classical town, such as Edinburgh (*128a, b*) or Bath is to enter quite another environment. Here is a different use of size, employing a spacious scale of measurement, founded on the classical ideal of perfection in proportion. It is seen at its best in buildings designed by Robert Adam (*128b*). This is to experience the grace and power of another set of values; 'experience' is used advisedly, for one seems not so much to notice satisfying sizes as to feel their effect.

There are, alas, in every part of the country ill-conceived bungalow developments which evoke feelings of absence of plan. This is the result of quite haphazard use of ground measurement, and badly arranged monotonous units, creating a dull, irritating effect. Much can be learned about proportion by being sensitive to one's environment, and asking, 'Why does this satisfy and that annoy?'

Other arts, such as graphic design and fashion make bold use of contrast in size to arrest attention, in poster design, for instance, and in garments which seem to change the shape of the human figure. Every abstract artist is seeking to express his ideas and feelings by using quantities in relation to each other, visually weighing and measuring one line against another, one shape against another. He is fascinated by forms (*96*), which in themselves may have strange proportions. These visual values are for him as sounds are to the musician—he composes with them. If he is a sculptor, he may be seeking to perfect, according to his own ideas, one single shape, one three-dimensional form, which contains within it many comparisons of size. A simple cubic form requires only one measurement each for height, width, and depth, but in one that is irregular and full of dramatic variation and subtlety, many calculations are needed for each dimension.

Proportion in modern building   (a)
127a Office blocks

127b The Adam Smith Building, Glasgow University.
Architects: David Harvey, Alexander Scott & Associates.
Photograph: Malcolm Hill

Edinburgh's classical New Town, 200 years old (facing)
128a Danube Street

128b North side of Charlotte Square. Designer: Robert
Adam. Photographs: courtesy Scottish Field   (b)

129a

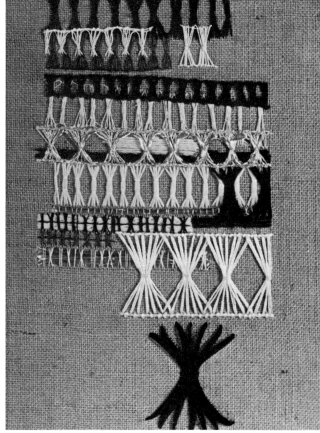

129b

130a

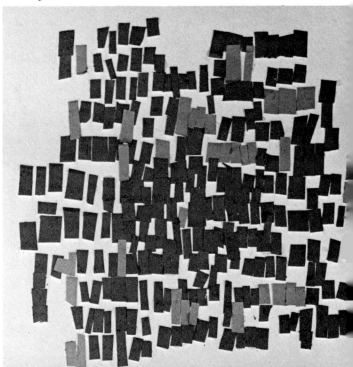

'Changing scale'. One-stitch exercise. Idea from looking at girders, which suggested sheaf stitch

129a Strips of girder pattern cut from newsprint plan a design, simplified in the embroidery to emphasise change of scale

129b Sheaf stitch variations in various kinds of black and white threads and silver knitting yarn. See also 21a

Mean proportion. Play on slight variation in size

130a Design for sheaf stitch sampler from small rectangles of red and crimson paper

130b Embroidery in a variety of reds, using sheaf stitch and buttonhole stitch variations, interprets the design, with more thought for balance and arrangement of colour, tone, and types of thread   Jennifer Marriot, Third Year

131 Part of student's Diploma Show. Panel on wall inspired by visiting exhibition of kinetic art. Grey background cut to show recessed area of black and white closely related shapes, which by their proportional variation and arrangement create an illusion of movement. (Property of Mr F. H. K. Henrion, M.B.E., R.D.I.)
                    Edmere Dalgliesh, Diploma Test

130b   131

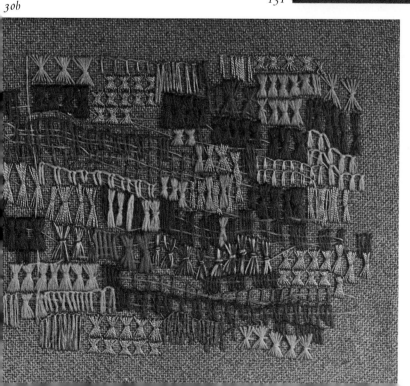

159

132 Stripes show contrast in width, tone, and plain to pattern

In a much simpler way, an embroidery designer, drawing or cutting shapes in paper or cloth, can be faced with the problem of deciding why a certain shape is dull, why it neither satisfies nor excites. It may be that it is indeterminate because its proportions have not been fully considered. It can be changed, however, its measurements reconsidered in relation to each other, and its appearance improved. Its outlines may lack interest, particularly in the case of irregular shapes, where the length of one straight edge to another must be carefully considered (*149*). Curved edges too require attention, whether they be of a gently waving nature, or full of frills like a petunia (*97, 121*). Occasionally in embroidery one sees heavy surface cords or threads that curve about in a meaningless manner. No thought has been given to the kind of curves they are making, nor to their comparative sizes, and this thoughtless feeling is apparent.

Some workers have a more highly developed sense of proportion than others, but even they can fall into the habit, unthinking as handwriting, of using the same proportions again and again, neglecting the very thing by which they can change the character of their design at will. The injunction 'to develop a sense of proportion' may sound like a Victorian maxim, but the designer who follows it will find she has a built-in visual yardstick.

Opportunity in proportion

LOOK AT BUILDINGS
—for comparative sizes in:
  outline shape;
  window pattern;
  doors and windows to frontage.
—for general atmosphere of environment.

EXERCISES
—using white paper, black paper, and newsprint:
  make stripes;
  make skyscraper window patterns (this can be done by weaving long strips of paper through each other);
  develop the idea from 'net' exercise (*126*), varying sizes by numbers, to study effects.

COLLECT STRIPED MATERIALS
—analyse their proportions.

WORDS CAN SUGGEST PROPORTION
—elegant, squat, dull, etc.
Study the appearance of household and other articles, and find words to describe their proportions.
Cut shapes suggested by the words.

EMBROIDERY
—choose a stitch as a motif for variation in size (*129, 130*).

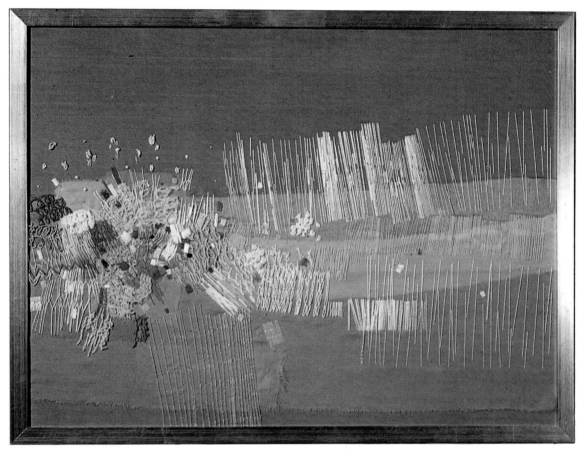

Plate 4 Spring, *26″ × 17″. Striped background shows motionless simplicity of earth. Swirling shapes, by contrast, reveal the sudden explosion of nature. Silk and wool stitchery on shantung and chiffon*   Linda Huck, Diploma Test

Colour and tone

Embroidery is fortunate to work in prepared colour, creating its effects from threads and fabrics dyed in kaleidoscopic variety—wools, silks, cottons, and synthetics, ranging from pale through brilliant to very dark tones—and all with their different textural characteristics which accentuate tonal variety.

Colour should be taught by contagion in an atmosphere of enthusiasm. It is very important to enjoy colour—at first any shades which the student happens to like, then gradually extending the palette by perception, finding colour in the whole of life. Everything has colour—not necessarily strong, easily distinguishable colour, but often strange muted fascinating mixtures which almost defy description. When one tries to convey what they look like in ordinary words, one has to do it by analysing their ingredients, and describing them as a 'whitish grey-green', or 'soft mauvish pink', or 'greyish putty colour'.

Curiosity about the composition of pigments, how to mix paints, or what constituent dyes have been used, is an admirable starting-point from which to study colour, sending the student directly to the spectrum and simple colour theory as points of reference. Theories about colour can be highly scientific and academic, but all that is necessary here is to provide sufficient knowledge to help the student's natural 'eye for colour', and provide a working basis for the understanding of family relationships in colour, and the use of tone. It is good to make a colour-wheel once in a lifetime, and thereafter to live, as it were, with a rainbow in the mind's eye.

Imagine the colours of the spectrum arranged in a fairly large ring of pure colours, each in turn merging into the next, with a strong pure red at the top. Let the eye travel clockwise, and the red gradually becomes vermilion, then orange. Losing its warmth, orange becomes yellow, a pure yellow which acquires a greenish tinge, turning to lime, and then becoming a strong green at the base of the ring, exactly opposite to red. Moving up to the left, green takes on a bluish tinge, becomes turquoise, then pure blue, which in turn grows warm, becoming violet, then purple, and through magenta back to red at the top. This is an almost casual impression of the spectrum colours, but sufficient to establish their sequence.

Now they can be considered in another way—red, yellow, and blue are called primary colours: each in its pure state contains nothing of the other two. Each is separate and quite different in composition. These three primary colours are found in the ring at points equidistant from each other, red at the top, yellow at four o'clock, and blue at eight o'clock. From these points of concentration, each colour spreads its influence to either side, red moving towards blue on the left and yellow on the right, yellow towards red and blue, and blue towards yellow and red. Where each pair meets, a new concentration of colour is found. Blue and yellow meet to form green, which is opposite to red, both in position at the base of the ring, and in composition. Since neither blue nor yellow has any tinge of red in its make-up, green can have none either. So red and green are completely different from each other. This is why they are commonly used as signals—they cannot be mistaken for each other. In the same manner orange is opposite to blue, and purple to yellow. These three colours—orange, green, and purple—are called secondary colours, and it is now established that there are six main colour areas in the ring of pure colour. Each of these areas contains many varieties of the one colour—red, for instance, being a family name for all shades grading from blue-reds (magenta and cerise) to the yellow-reds (scarlet and vermilion).

Each family is, however, very much larger than the part of it which lies within the ring of pure colour. These strong colours can lose their concentration and become paler, and they can also become darker in tone. Let the eye look again at the ring of pure colour, and draw in from it towards the centre of the circle. The colours, as if lightened by the addition of white, grow gradually paler and paler, until they finally converge at pure white in the centre. Then let the eye travel outwards from the pure colour-ring, and each colour will grow deeper and deeper in tone, as if mixed with black, until the outer ring is one of complete black.

This is now a large and informative circle, in which it is possible to trace the tonal path of each colour along a radial line, from very pale in the centre, through pure colour, to very dark at the outer edge. As an example, white can become the palest shell-pink, gather strength through varying degrees of salmon-pink to pure scarlet, then deepen to rust, grow reddish brown, and finally become a brown-black. Examples of other gradations are—pale primrose to yellow, then khaki; ice-pink to magenta, then maroon; duck-egg blue to turquoise, then a dark green-blue.

These are examples of simple tone variations on pure colour, but most of the colours we encounter are the result of highly complex mixtures of pigments or dyes, and involve combining opposite colours in various ways. If a pot of red paint is far too strident, it can be almost imperceptibly subdued by adding a few drops of green, and in the same way a very subtle green can be got by reducing its original harshness with red.

In a material like Harris tweed actual variously coloured fibres can be observed. They are combed or carded together before spinning, and lie in such close association that their original hues are cancelled out to produce what is called a 'neutral-coloured' material—one which is too indeterminate in colour to belong to any one family. This is exactly what happens in paint when the three primary colours are mixed together. The potencies of red, blue, and yellow reduce each other, and are said to produce grey.

In fact, they create all sorts of subtleties depending on their proportions —cool greys when blue predominates, buff shades leading to browns when red is stronger, and greenish-khaki colours when there is most of yellow.

Shot materials, with warp of one shade crossing weft of another, can have wonderfully vibrant effects, particularly when the colours are strong and close in tone. Thai silk, for instance, crosses scarlet with bright sweet pink (*Plate 8*). Other good examples of direct colour mixing in fabrics can be found in plaids and tartans, where many different shades of yarn cross each other in great variety.

Nature is a wonderful storehouse of colour, both in the wide prospect and in detail. The soil changes its colour from one district to another, showing red, brown, grey, or white. Certain things like fungus and tree bark suggest tone as much as colour, so also do shells at the light end of the scale. Rose catalogues make wonderful reading for the colour conscious. Such phrases as 'scarlet suffused mauve' can only be excelled by the flowers themselves.

Seeing colour becomes a major preoccupation, noticing its effect in an environment. A bright new scheme of colour can transform an urban area, while old weather-beaten pieces of colour have their own attraction, especially for such artists as Utrillo and John Piper.

Light constantly plays a strong part. Early morning light can transform a green tree into pure gold. Strong sunlight tends to bleach colour, producing a general feeling of lightness, accentuated by the strong tonal contrast of shadows. Clouds sweeping across the sun create huge moving patterns of dark purple-green on moorland hills, and reflected light at sunset warms the land and turns it brownish pink.

One delights also in brightly coloured clothes, and the enchanting accidental schemes which form as people meet and congregate, from the dazzling pointillist effect of a crowd gathered in a Spanish arena, to the muted blues, purples, and faint mauves worn by a gang of workmen wearing well-washed and faded jeans.

All these experiences provide impetus towards working in colour, and creating schemes of individual choice. Embroidery provides the perfect medium, and the purpose. It is imperative that all old clichés and taboos should be banished, such as the idea that a certain colour does not 'go' with another. Each shade must be seen freshly, as it is, and related as far as possible to its source in the spectrum colour-ring, in order to know about it and find agreeable companions for it. Reference to the spectrum suggests simple methods of associating colour, and, although all theories are mere pointers, the following ideas may be helpful.

Most flags and banners find their colours almost entirely from the ring

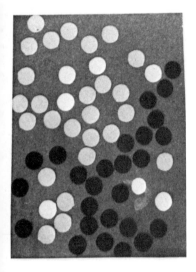

of pure colour—reds, greens, blues, and yellows. A bunch of sweet-peas in creams, pinks, blues, and mauves takes its pale colouring from the central part of the circle—they are often called 'pastel shades'. A sombre scheme of dark blues, browns, and purples, as in a winter coat material, finds its colours near the outer rim. These are three examples of multi-colour schemes in which there is little or no contrast in tone. Tone remains fairly constant while colour varies. The very opposite is found in a mono-chromatic scheme where within one colour family there may be a great deal of tonal variation—a multiplicity of varied reds and pinks for instance.

Colours are said to be in harmony when they follow in sequence, as in the spectrum. A green-blue range could have tonal variations thus—bottle-green, turquoise, deep blue, and hyacinth-mauve.

Contrasting colours are those which are found opposite in the circle—reds and greens, blues and oranges, and purples and yellows. If these are used together in their purest forms, and in equal quantities, they create a dazzling effect, as in some striped materials and in modern kinetic painting. Very beautiful schemes of contrast can be evolved by balancing tones and considering quantities, for example—purples and mauves with strange greenish and khaki yellows. Many satisfactory schemes are built on a subtle interpretation of the primary colours, such as—Indian red, Wedg-wood blue, and dull gold; or geranium-pink, navy, and lemon-yellow. Dazzling contrasts have already been mentioned, but there are also close-toned, closely related pairs of colours which vibrate when used together—scarlet and bright pink, lemon-yellow and yellow-ochre, emerald-green and turquoise-blue, to name a few. These pungencies can form highlights in a colour scheme, backed up by subdued and deeper shades.

In embroidery, background colour is of the greatest importance. It must entice the student to work on it. It cannot be said that any one colour is better than another. Some are much easier to work on, and each needs individual consideration when choosing the colour scheme of threads and materials to use with it. The idea that a neutral background has 'no colour' is quite wrong; it is a subtle mixture and, like all the greys, khakis, and 'off' colours, provides an interesting base when well used. These compli-cated shades have been derived from many colours, and so they have natural affinities to these colours, as well as being subdued contrasts to others. This is why they make very good grounds.

Pure colour, such as strong yellow, makes a splendid background for a tonal scheme of blacks, greys, and whites (*Plate 7*), or for bold contrast of reds and blues, but the enticing idea of using yellows on yellow is found to be more difficult, since the background colour subtracts its own

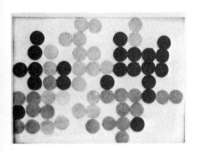

133 Monochrome photographs reveal the tone values in colour exercises

potency of yellow from that of each thread used on it. The exercise becomes a struggle, often very worth while, to manipulate tone and texture within the yellow family (*135*).

Colours constantly affect each other, enhancing or cancelling, and a piece of individual background colour, which in itself is exciting or satisfying, cannot remain unaffected; it changes as other colour is related to it. This is the thrilling part of creating in colour—observing the reactions of one shade to another, and trying to control the effect by quantity, position, intensity, and tone. Contrast, proportion, and balance are as important here as in the other aspects of design, whether the plan be for a large, telling simplicity, or for a dazzling, pointillist effect, where brilliance is the sum of broken colour supported by shadow.

Opportunity in colour and tone

Become very aware of colour.
Notice both natural arrangements and man-made schemes.

SPECTRUM
Make a colour-wheel as suggested in the text, or devise original methods for forming simple colour and tone gradations. For an embroiderer it is actually more useful to collect and organise scraps of fabric out of delight in their appearance, than to attempt to get complete theoretical exactness of shade and tone in paint.

COLLECT
—shade cards of all kinds—artist's colours, house paints, embroidery threads, knitting wools, etc., and study their particular selections.
—pieces of coloured paper. Advertisement pages in magazines provide some splendid colour, usually with good tonal contrast. Cut these up and use them for schemes, and for planning designs. Chance can play a part here—for instance, how many blues can be found in one magazine?
For semi-transparent experiments use coloured tissue papers, and observe colour changes in opposites—pink on green, yellow on mauve, etc. This makes a good introduction to experiments with transparent materials— tarlatans, chiffons, and organdies.
—snippets of every kind of material, and keep them in glass jars according to their colour families. The variety in each jar will be amazing, and many shades will almost defy classification. These collections can be used to plan schemes on differently toned backgrounds—light, medium, and dark.

CREATE
—multicolour schemes within a close tone range.
—monochrome schemes using many varieties of one colour.
—primary schemes, and secondary schemes, both bold and subtle.
—harmonies.
—contrasts.
—schemes derived from nature—from shells, flowers, etc.
—gay schemes (*Plate 4*).
—sombre schemes (*Plate 5*).

ANALYSIS
Obtain patterns of tweeds in good colour varieties. Note the proportions of the various colours and shades to each other.

EMBROIDERY
Work small sample pieces of embroidery, using various kinds of thread, to try out colour schemes.

Close, flat stitchery gives the maximum value to coloured thread against the background.

Open lace-like stitchery creates broken colour in conjunction with the background.

Ranges of colour and tone can be achieved by working interlocking rows of one stitch, such as blanket or herringbone. This produces shading, which is a very old device, but, like others, it can be used in new ways.

Develop stitch patterns to display colour.

Use materials in patches to build up larger areas of colour.

Watch all effects and profit from each experiment.

134 Spring, *28″ × 34″. This panel achieves its effect of vitality and upsurge of growth by its design, use of stitchery, and quite non-literal use of colour. The background is a quiet mauve rayon with a mat surface. Full round threads make natural stitch shapes in almost primitive reds, purples, and lemon-yellows, interspersed with flat thready areas in a variety of soft grey-greens. The palm-leaf shapes at the top provide contrast in form and technique. Long straight stitches of pure silk in soft greens and delicate pinks achieve maximum light-catching effect*
Agnes Hamilton, Diploma Test

135 Daffodils, 24″ × 40″. Detail from panel in a monochromatic colour scheme of yellow. Background of light yellow woollen material. Embroidery uses varied woollen threads in ranges from white to strong pure yellow, cream to warm yellows, and orange-buff shades with dark ochre, tan, and raw umber

Linda Huck, Third Year

136 Detail of corn from Communion Table scarf, showing light and shade in gold embroidery, a dramatic effect necessary in Church work to be seen from a distance. Heads of corn prepared individually, using gold kid, metal threads, and sequins in a variety of patterns suggested by corn, padded and applied to the strong green-gold background. Stems and beards worked later. (Property of Allan Park Church, Stirling)   Hannah Frew

Plate 5 Second Symphony of Sibelius, *30″ × 19″. Design conceived by listening to the music. Vigorous stitchery at the top conveys excitement; textural band of materials, Finland; blacks and greys, brooding feeling of the music; plain areas, serenity*
Margaret Allan, Diploma Test

Using fabrics—texture

Embroidery is a textural art. The word 'texture' means literally 'something woven', but has come to denote surface quality in the widest sense—something recognisable not only by the eye, but closely involving the sense of touch. Handling materials is one of the surest ways of recognising their basic substance, as well as of determining their quality.

Every embroiderer amasses pieces of material for the sheer joy of possessing them—for their inspiration, and the enticement they provide towards starting new work. Simple materials, such as linen scrims and hopsacks have already been mentioned as being suitable backgrounds for early work, and cloths specially manufactured for traditional embroideries have also been referred to. Today, however, there are so many beautiful fabrics that, provided the choice is a wise one for the work to be undertaken, any type of material can be used. All simply woven fabrics with a hand-spun quality make excellent backgrounds, for instance—self-coloured Donegal tweed, Thailand silk, rough Indian cotton, and many linens in the furnishing range, particularly if the colours are natural or muted in tone. The natural appearance of these materials makes them particularly ready to take hand embroidery, with its threads and stitches merging and becoming embedded into warp and weft in a very satisfactory way.

Other fabrics develop different relationships with stitchery. On a close, smooth material, for instance, embroidery can tend to appear repoussé—to sit almost independently on the surface of the cloth. An obvious weave pattern, even a simple twill, can be slightly distracting to the worker, and a herringbone pattern even more so. Fancy weaves, such as basket effects, begin to set up a tension between the original pattern in the cloth and the worker's intention for the stitchery. One solution is to make the work sufficiently strong in scale of thread and stitch to combat the disturbing effect of the ground; another is to derive ideas from the woven texture itself, which influence the choice of stitches. Herringbone, chevron, Cretan, and fly stitches can very effectively echo herringbones, diamond patterns, and twills in the structure of the fabric. If the woven pattern is very insistent, as in the case of a bold checked linen, the embroidery must complement it and become an adjunct to the basic design (*142*). These instances serve to show how necessary it is to consider well the relationship between stitches and material.

In average circumstances it is unwise to choose a material with an extreme texture as a background—fur fabrics, for instance, at one end of the scale, and satin or plastic at the other. Such extremes of rough and smooth would bring the work into the category of 'special problems', which mature designers evolve for the pleasure of solving them (*166*).

Cloth supplies, not only backgrounds, but also a whole range of 'raw materials' from which to create fabric embroideries, and although it is so readily obtainable and in such common use, it is in this context a medium of expression, and merits some consideration before one starts to use it in this special way.

It would be useful at this point to think about the complete range of available textiles. The fabric department of any large store displays a wide selection of materials, each in its own colour range, but this represents a mere fraction of the whole, when one considers, for instance, the number and diversity of textile articles necessary for the comfort of any one person in a single day. Each room in the house has its own appurtenances—a variety of kitchen cloths, linen and terry towels in the bathroom, table linen, everything for a bed, upholstery materials, curtains and carpets of very many kinds—these are all grouped as furnishing textiles. Dress textiles present an even larger array of woven, knitted, and fabricated stuffs, suitable for making upper and under, outdoor and indoor, working and playing, day, evening, and night clothes for men, women, and children. To think about this, gives some slight idea of the magnitude of the textile industry, but it also conveys the fact that each fabric has its own use and separate characteristics—its own texture. Old and ordinary things can be just as interesting as grand and special materials, particularly when embroidery provides them with a new use, and they acquire a fresh interest through being seen out of their normal context.

With such a vast range of possible materials to choose from—even if the worker is relying modestly on the rag-bag for her initial supply of pieces—it becomes clear that a method must be devised to help her to find her way in texture, no less than in colour. She must have opportunities to handle, examine, compare, and generally take note of fabrics, in order to develop a textile sense, which is something latent in everyone. It is immensely satisfying and instructive to make organised collections of fabrics (*140e*), arranging them at first like sample cards, according to their kinds:—for instance:

Cottons—fine to rough: muslins, organdies, tarlatans, shirtings, sheetings, fancy weaves, towelling, etc.

Silks—dull to lustrous: raw silk, Thailand silk, spun silk, Japanese silk, faille, corded silk, and satin.

Wools—thin to thick: nun's veiling, flannel, dress wools (including crêpes), all weights of tweed in plain and twill weaves, up to the thickest Harris and heavy coat materials.

Since this is a fascinating pursuit, the worker will see that arranging according to kind is only a start, and will be able to think of other criteria, such as 'quality', and arrange the pieces in a gradation of 'poor to rich' (scrim to lamé), for example. She will also begin to develop ideas for interesting textural schemes in the same way as one creates colour schemes. There is a definite analogy between colour and texture, which can be most easily appreciated when working or thinking in monochrome. Deep pile materials seem to correspond to dark tones, dull surface medium weights to subdued colour, light materials to clear colour, and high gloss fabrics to brilliant hues. A texture scheme needs all the consideration of variety and balance in arranging its surfaces, that a satisfactory colour scheme requires in handling its tones. This analogy is useful, for when one thinks about it, colour and texture are inseparably linked. Every piece of fabric has some recognisable colour, even if it is an undyed 'dirty white', and texture creates further colour variation. If several different materials are all dyed to the same intensity of a colour, they will each appear slightly different, due to their surfaces absorbing and reflecting light differently.

This unlimited diversity of colour and texture provides vast scope for working in materials. At the outset, it is possible to make quite unsatisfactory mixtures, due usually to ignorance of quality, too hasty choice, having too few fabrics from which to select, or using far too many different kinds. Another pitfall is the temptation to choose for the sake of colour alone without due regard to texture, colour usually being the more eye-catching of the two qualities. Once more the art of choice is in operation, and the worker has the basic concepts of affinity, contrast, and proportion to guide her in creating colour and texture schemes.

A useful preliminary exercise would be to select pairs of textures which seem to complement each other, such as felt (which is very smooth) on hessian, with its obvious weave. The student could then choose three or four contrasting surfaces, and use each one as the beginning of a gradation, so that finally several textural themes are involved in the one exercise. To explain further—hessian's main characteristic is its weave, and the same quality with different scale and texture is found in rough linen, and also in furnishing and other fabrics which are based on a plain weave structure: the feeling of vertical and horizontal warp and weft is common to all, although they vary in scale and substance. Felt has two characteristics—it is smooth, and woollen. Its woollen nature leads it towards flannel, smooth dress weights, and even to crêpes, while its smoothness suggests dull silk, shiny rayon, and even plastic. This is very theoretical, but it is the type of thought plan to have in mind. Although at this stage experiment and personal discovery are all-important, it is wise to evolve simple fabric affinity schemes, so as to avoid discouragement through muddle.

Some workers have an instinctive gift for using texture; others find it a help to have definite subject-matter as a starting-point. Although finding

137 and 138 Rapid fabric exercises on black muslin create ▶
an opportunity to handle and experiment with materials
Second Year

the right scrap of fabric for some concrete idea such as fish scales is exciting, a more useful kind of subject-matter in this context is one suggesting a colour and texture atmosphere only, and titles such as 'Blue Haze', 'Green Shade', or 'Golden Glory' might inspire interesting schemes.

Exploiting fabrics as 'raw material' is no new thing. The aim in doing traditional patchwork, as we have seen, is to use old and odd materials to make a completely new and durable fabric structure, and at the same time to exploit the pattern content of the original materials, creating new design. In appliqué, as the name suggests, areas of fabric are applied to a background, to supply colour and surface variation, usually sewn down very precisely, making a neat, strong finished edge. This is a technique which is often employed in Church work, which is subject to constant use (*178*, *179*). 'Fabric collage' can mean a design built up with areas of material, either by sticking them to a background, or by stitching them down in a mechanical or very basic manner, the stitching playing no intended part in the design (*149*). Where stitchery is used in a manner intended to complement the areas of material, supplying further colour and texture, it would seem the term 'collage' is a misnomer, and the work should simply be called an 'embroidery' (*Plates 4 and 5*).

So far, the application of materials has been referred to as creating areas of texture and colour, but it would be limiting to regard this as the only way of using fabrics. It is a matter of experiment and discovery to put materials to a new use: to find methods of changing their structure and relating them one to another in different ways. Reducing a fabric by drawing out various warp and weft strands, and then tying its floating threads in bunches with stitches, is usually associated with the specialised even-weave linen techniques, drawn thread work, and drawn fabric (*42–44*). Although usually employed on household articles, these techniques have decorative possibilities far beyond the traditional uses, and can be exploited to create transparent, lace-like embroideries, which appear like freely controlled arrangements of holes, bunches, fringes, and loops (*45a*). Furthermore, these ideas need not be confined to linens and even-weaves, but can be used to change the density of any material, from tweed (by pulling out areas of its warp and weft) to nylon stockings (by laddering them). Breaking up a material in this way makes it lighter in appearance, gives it better relationship to its background, and enhances its intrinsic quality by discovering the yarns from which it is woven. Broken materials can take on new shapes and characteristics (*140c*).

The superimposing of transparent materials, such as organdies, tarlatans, and chiffons, has a similarity to print-making in its overlays of colour, and can provide additional possibilities for trapping sequins and other small facet effects between layers (*Plate 6*). Pliable materials can be pleated (*141*), folded, gathered, and organised, even torn in strips and used as thread, to make soft three-dimensional effects against a background.

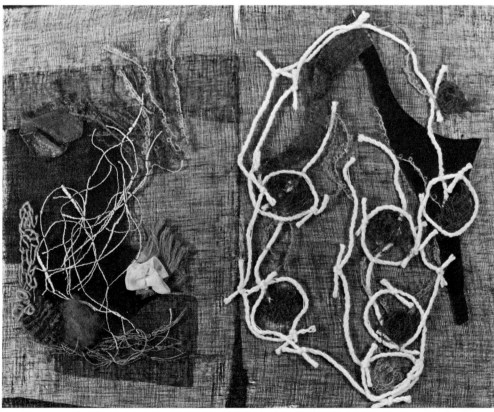

In experimenting to find new ways of using fabrics, design and technique must be very closely associated. A new technique can make possible a special interpretation of a design (*145*).

A very important aspect of using materials, and one sometimes ignored, is the treatment of edges, each of which is a line delineating a shape, each with positive value in the finished work. Different treatments result in entirely different edge effects. Materials may be torn, cut neatly, hacked, turned in and hemmed, left raw but fixed evenly, fringed, or frayed. A shape may be surrounded by a tight line which will isolate it, or lightly fixed with a variable stitch, decorated with beads, or merged by shading into its surroundings. The possible effects are many and varied.

Quilting, padding, making boxes, and similar activities have always provided an element of the third dimension in embroidery, heightening the qualities of the materials by allowing an added play of light and shade. This is another fascinating point for development, with the proviso that experiment should aim to enhance the original surface effects of the material (*170 and Plate 8*).

Opportunity in fabrics

COLLECT MATERIALS AND DELIGHT IN THEM
Organise them according to their raw materials, types of construction, and surface qualities.
Devise ideas for ranges and categories, for example:
aristocrats—pure silks, linens, hand-spun cottons, finest wools. These provide a standard of excellence.
exciting synthetics—compare them with their natural models. Some are made to resemble natural materials, others are frankly synthetic and have a special quality, the crystal nylons for example.
plastics—non-woven sheetings in brilliant colours, golds and silvers.
knitted fabrics—hand and machine made, from 'big pin' to nylon stockings.
'three-dimensional' materials—plush, quilting, etc.
nets—wedding-veil, strawberry-nets, fish-nets.
laces and meshes.
leathers and kids.

139 Designing with fabrics: exercises in proportion. Brilliantly coloured 'tiles' could serve as ideas for larger work, perhaps Church embroidery   Elise Curr, Fourth Year

Select pairs of complementary textures and build on these as suggested in the text.

Chequer-board designs
    (1) Monochrome—various textiles in white, black, or colour.
    (2) Polychrome—similar textures in a harmonious colour scheme.

Disintegrating exercise
    Using tweed, or loosely woven pieces, decompose them in part or entirely. Use the yarns and fragments to make a new arrangement on a thin background. This can make a 'temporary tapestry'.

'Ladders' exercise (140c).

Edges exercise
    (1) Create a pattern of overlapping fringes, etc.
    (2) Make a pattern incorporating fraying, folding, and fringes.

Try all kinds of experimenting, but do not incorporate more than one or two ideas in an exercise; they may kill each other.

140a Material exercise in black and white, 14″ square, using cylindrical shapes of varying heights
Magdalene Carnegie, Third Year

140d

140b

140b Pheasant. *Strips of material, pieces of tweed, stocking, multiple yarns, etc., used in bold textural stitchery. Hot colours*   Daphne Fitzgerald, Third Year

140c *Detail of shredded and broken materials. See page 174*

140d Banner. *Fabric experiment in blues and pinks, using plaited and twisted rayons and cotton*
          Jennifer Marriot, Third Year

140e *Fabric exercise. Collecting and organising materials for texture and colour. See page 170*

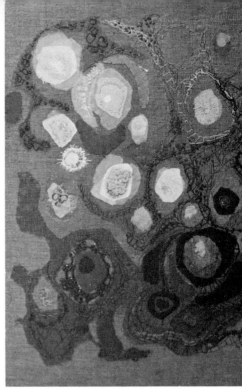

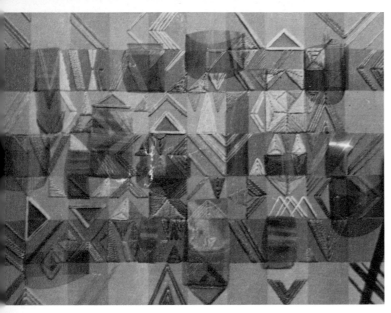

Growth rhythms in materials
143a Good tonal arrangements of materials and stitchery   Second Y

143b Brilliant pinks and black, with a chain of knotted gold and sequins   Jill Gerber, Second Y

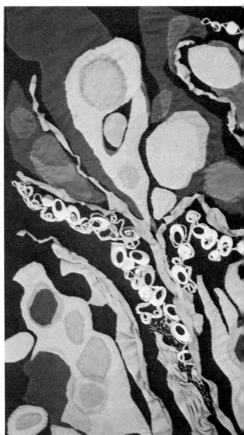

141 Experimental panel, 10″ × 15″, using pleated chiffon. Wafting shapes offset by straight bands of threads
Margaret Allan, Third Year

142 Checked background enriched by geometric stitchery pattern, using coton perlé, stranded cotton, and silk threads in straight stitches. Colours range from yellows and various shades of orange to vermilion and mauves. Work further enhanced by the use of cinnamoid in flat areas and hoops, creating a diffuse colour effect, 15″ × 11″
Fiona McGeachy, Fourth Year

144 The Sea, *a hanging,* *32″ × 72″*. *Free rhythmical*
shapes cut from fabrics of varied texture and transparency,
in shades of khaki, dark green, purple, brilliant yellow,
and blue, with pendant cinnamoid fish. The sun is crotcheted
from strips of yellow tarlatan with gold additions
Margaret Allan, Fourth Year

145a Panel based on a painting of flowers, 34" × 45". A completely abstract use of threads and materials convey the worker's feeling for the subject, with something of the quality of a musical tone poem in strange pinks, cold mauves, and gold. The background is dull pink woollen material, and the stitchery varies from very fine in silk and French gold to very large using strips of chiffon as thread
Agnes Hamilton, Fourth Year

145b Detail ▶

147 Night Flower, *11″ × 24″*. *New substances such as cinnamoid make effective contributions to the range of materials for embroidery. Panel on a black background, using grey cinnamoid, silver and white stitchery with pearls. Photograph: courtesy Scottish Design Centre*

Janet Boyd

◀ 146 Four Hearts, *24″ × 36″*. *Felt inlay on purple hessian, using purples, reds, and white, with gold kid and fine gold line. Photograph: courtesy Scottish Design Centre*

Janet Boyd

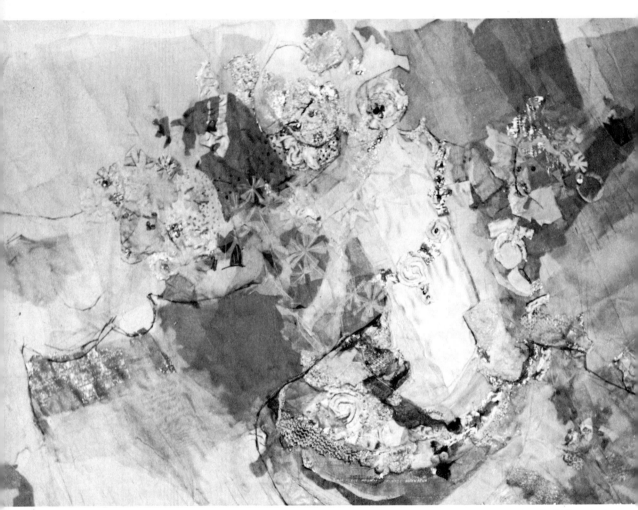

148 *Detail of Plate 6*

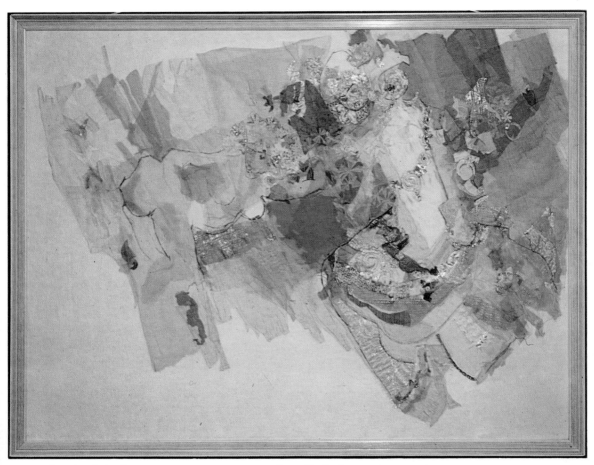

Plate 6 Fabric Composition, *30″ × 45″. On white silk, built up in layers and folds of chiffon and other transparencies to rich concentrations of texture and intricate design. Rich fabrics, sequins, etc. combine with fine line to indicate figures, on which the idea of the design is based. The composition seems to float across the area*   *Kirsty Davidson, Fourth Year*

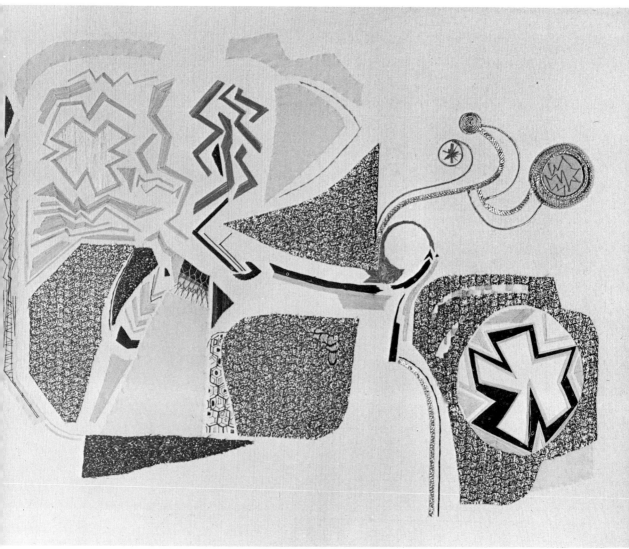

*149 Panel, 28" × 38". Design based on the idea of mach-
inery, with clean-cut forms and hard edges. White ground,
with yellow, silver, turquoise, and black materials*
                                    Jan Machesney

150 Blue Gothic, *18″ × 24″. Panel in fine materials—
nylons, transparent rayons, and chiffons in shades of blue
and grey, with a central motif of silver. Design a play on
arches and cut edges   Maureen Spence, Fourth Year*

Composition

Composition comes as a climax to this investigation. It is a synthesis, bringing together in practice the various processes of embroidery and aspects of design which have been considered separately. It must make use of materials and colour, consider ways of working, rely on drawing, and be continuously aware of contrast in line, shape, and pattern; as well as all these things it requires some additional investigation into design.

In setting out to make a panel of embroidery, two aspects of design must be kept continually in mind—the small and the large. The work will display an invention of threads and materials, creating a rich surface—this aspect has already been stressed, but it must also show evidence of planning, to achieve a totality and have impact. It is most important that a piece of decoration which will, in all probability, be seen on a wall, should have the power, firstly to arrest attention, and then on closer inspection to reveal the intricacy and beauty of the work which has gone into its creation. The designer's early vision should encompass a unity, however vaguely seen at the start, a finished whole with all its aspects working towards one essential simplicity of statement, rich in colour, texture, and invention. It involves firstly concentration on the large aspect of design, to obtain a satisfactory use of the whole background area, and to include opportunities for the further stages of development right up to the final intricacies. Embroidery can be thought of in layers. Its final result is often attained through building one effect upon another (173). This requires planning.

The first prickings of an idea for an embroidery can come in any number of ways—from handling materials, from a realisation of the creative possibilities of colour, from a technique, from something seen, or from an abstract idea—but no matter where the suggestion begins, the final work must take shape within a given area, usually a rectangle.

The rectangle is a necessary convention. Other shapes, such as circles (89, 90), ovals, or irregular forms can be used when desired, but the rectangle in all its variations is the universally accepted framework, and will be considered here. The problem it poses is that of making use of enclosed space, as opposed to the idea of unlimited space implicit in pattern design. This underlines a difference between designing 'in repeat', as for printed and woven textiles, and making one coherent statement within a given area for a panel of embroidery. Let us imagine the ground material stretched on an embroidery frame, neatly surrounded by folded paper so that the exact area of the finished composition is visible (*160c*). The first thing to do is to look at the area and appreciate the beauty of an undisturbed space, to notice its proportions, and realise that every part of it is important. If, for instance, a sheet of paper of similar size were cut into pieces and then reassembled, every piece would be required to make the original whole; so there will be no unimportant parts in the finished work on this ground. Some areas will eventually carry more interest than others, but they will be offset by the value of the plain spaces. A rectangle has four straight sides and four corners; these are important as boundaries to the design, and also as lines and angles seen in relation to the content of the design. It is very wrong to imagine that 'placing' on the background does not matter much because the frame will pull the whole thing together. In the case of a spot design within a rectangle, the proportion of background to design is very important (*91, 146*). This is, in fact, a basic compositional exercise, relating one kind of shape to another (*82*). If the spot is to look all-important, it will need little background (*Plate 7*), if an accent, it can appear, suitably placed, on a large area.

Composition can begin anywhere within the area. There is no rule which says that the design content should be placed in or near the centre of the rectangle. It can grow from the foot, enter from the side, infiltrate from a corner (*151–154*); choice is completely free, but the first step is very important, since all other arrangements are made in relation to it, and are conditioned by it.

Some simple and helpful effects can be observed by direct experiment. Let us return to the undisturbed area of coloured material, and break its surface by placing a spot of contrast upon it. The whole aspect is now changed; the eye focuses constantly upon the spot, while the surrounding area has most definitely become background. If another spot or shape is placed at a distance from the first, a feeling of tension is set up between the two, and the eye travels constantly from one to the other. If a third spot is added, the eye takes this in also. The first spot is now much less important, and the eye lingers on the one which attracts most attention, either because it is the largest in size, or the brightest in colour, or marked out by some eccentricity. Meanwhile, the background has become more broken up by having three spots placed on it, and the spaces between them are in need of consideration. If they seem unbalanced and awkward, then obviously the arrangement of the spots is bad. Their placing must be reconsidered in relation to each other, to the areas of background which are equally important parts of the composition, and to the rectangle as a whole. It becomes an exercise in proportion within the rectangle, to alter sizes, to vary tone and colour, and, since the word 'spot' is used in its widest sense, to change their shapes also. Constant observation of the results of these adjustments helps the worker to decide why some arrangements are more satisfactory to the eye than others. They can be bold through the use of strong contrast, or subtle through slight variation. Some arrangements have a satisfying simplicity, while others by their unexpectedness create excitement (*155*).

The following little illustration shows how relationships between shapes can change and affect each other:

The Policeman and the Boys On a vacant lot there is a large, sturdy, upstanding line—that is a policeman. At a short distance from him there is a dot—that is a boy. The line is important, and the dot insignificant. But another dot arrives beside the first, and more and more dots come running from all over the lot, and crowd together in a large, slightly menacing mass. Suddenly the policeman looks quite small.

These examples illustrate design evolving, as shapes are organised within the rectangle, and it goes without saying that, no matter what the shapes represent, the same rules of balance and contrast hold good: the shapes may be geometrical, or representational, or actual—arranging flower heads in a box, for instance.

Lines can be used to divide up an area in very many ways. They can run from one boundary to another, cutting the area completely and isolating parts from each other (in which case these parts must have satisfactory size and shape relationships). Lines can follow systems, running parallel, for instance, as illustrated in the proportion exercise (*126*), or rhythmical groupings, as in the composition inspired by the movement of water (*76*). It is often necessary to decide whether the composition is essentially of lines, or of shapes resulting from those lines. There develops in certain compositions a relationship between complete areas of design and equally complete areas of background; these are known as positive and negative form. *Spanish Bird* (*93*) is an illustration of this.

It is possible to give only a few signposts to composition here. Descriptions of the panels accompanying this chapter will help to make the subject more clear, and it will be appreciated that all the examples illustrated in the book have been planned, and are relevant to the subject. Much can be learned by studying them in the light of what has been said.

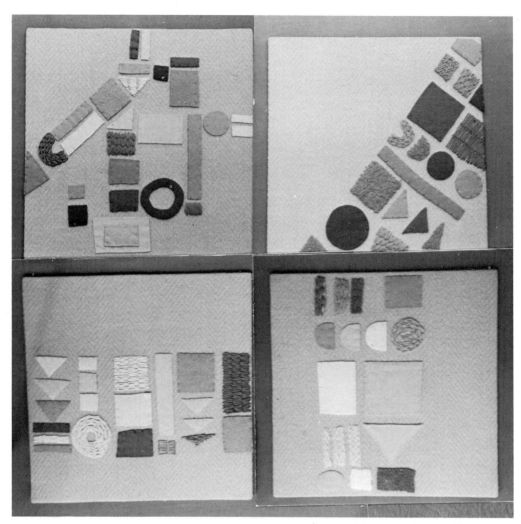

151 *Four simple geometric compositions within squares together form a balanced arrangement on a dark background. A horizontal band of pattern leads from the lower left to a vertical band of different width on the right. This moves upwards to a diagonal contrast of plain to pattern, from which a dark circle makes contact with a ring in the last square. Here horizontal and diagonal forces combine with vertical, which leads the eye back to the first square. Ten-inch squares of yellow on a dark blue ground, with pattern first in blues, then yellows, reds, and finally a combination of all three   Catriona Leslie, Fourth Year*

152 Composition, 48″ × 32″, built on a square grid, makes use of its original structure by a rectangular quality of outline, but departs from it by free geometric treatment within the squares. Well-controlled negative shapes of background act as a foil to the strong positive areas of texture, created in fabrics and stitchery. Brilliant colours on a white ground   *Mary Ward*

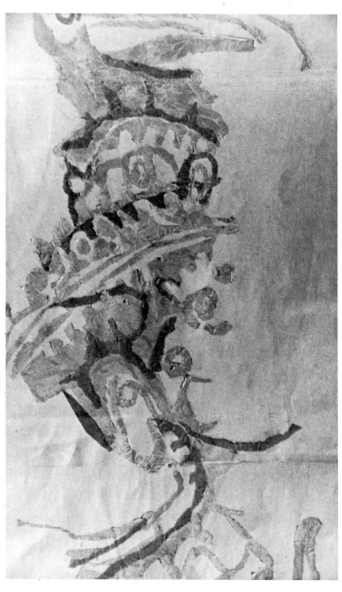

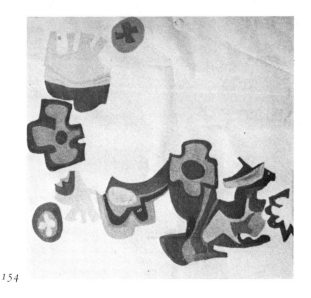

154

153a Design from growth form. Upward thrusting move-ment at base and on left, with contrasting aggressive movement entering from the right

153b Design based on a shell, in torn tissue paper and gum. Upward Spiralling movement

154 Design for stool-top in leather inlay. Shapes enter at the right, make a focal point, and move round and upwards to be effectively stopped by a cross within a circle

155 Square composition. Strong tension between tilted black square and erratic border of hieroglyph-like marks

155

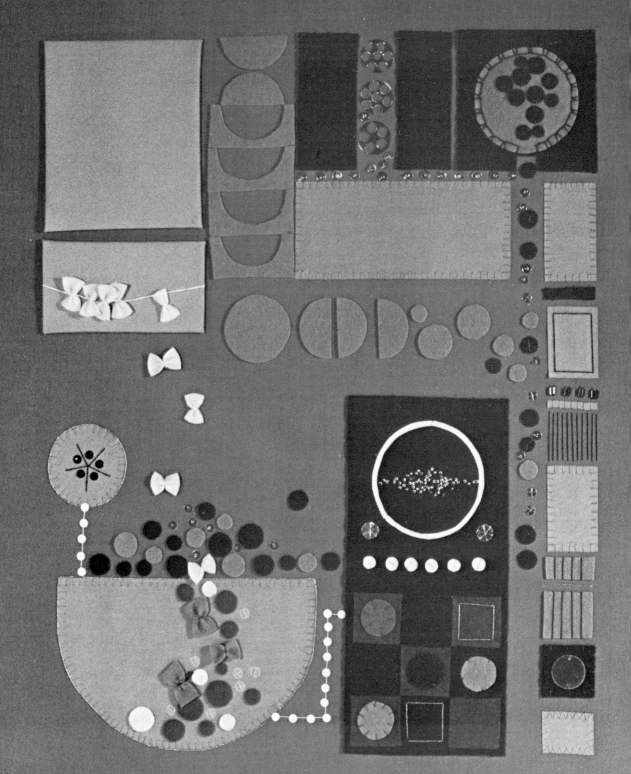

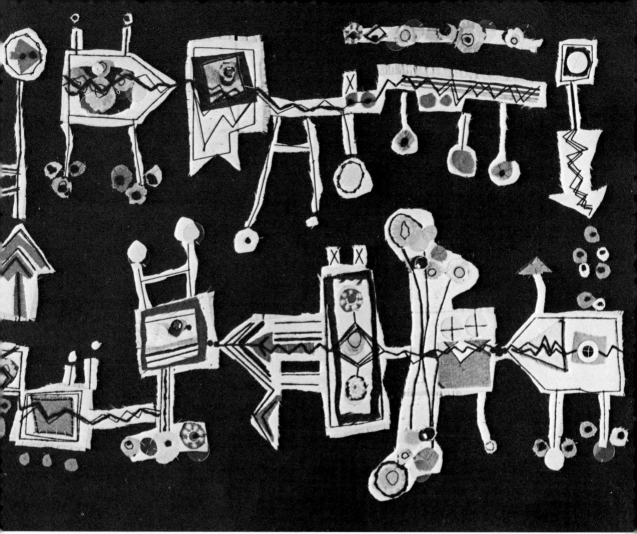

157 Gay Computer (2), *21″ × 16″. A more fantastic approach to the same subject. Procession of white cotton shapes seem to shunt round on inadequate wheels and meet opposition at the top. Black background, with white, and spots of gay colour—crimson, emerald-green, and orange*   *Margaret Allan, Third Year*

◀ 156 Gay Computer (1), *12″ × 16″. Composition of static geometric shapes incorporating liberal ideas of mechanical movement. Cross-currents of spots travel, become involved together, and pass on. Blue poplin ground, with shapes in navy, scarlet, various blues, and brilliant yellow*   *Agnes Hamilton, Third Year*

158a *Simple geometrical use of space for areas of rich stitchery. Camel-coloured cloth, 18″ × 45″, embroidered in natural shades from white to buff, with blue-green, light emerald, and soft orange*   Agnes Hamilton, Third Year

158b *Detail of stitchery* ▶

196

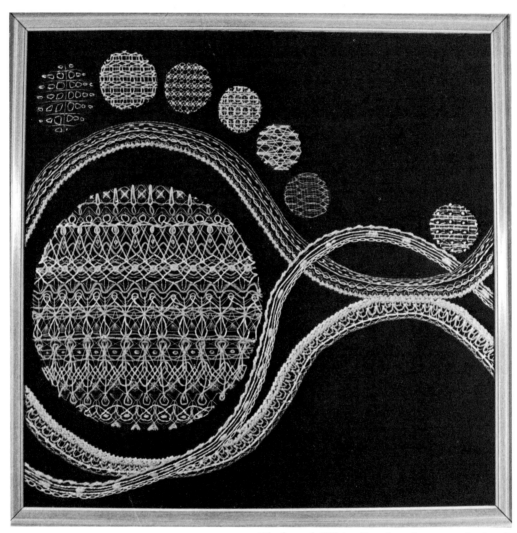

159 Black and White Panel, *27″ square. Intricately
worked circle rendered static by the horizontal feeling of its
pattern, held captive in the system of moving lines, and
balanced by the plain areas of background on the right.
Small circles create a broken curve and lead the eye to the
background. See also 109a and 109b for detail*

Marilyn McGregor

Stages in creating embroidery

It depends greatly on the temperament and ability of the designer, and also on the importance and type of work in hand, how far and in what manner designs are prepared prior to starting upon a piece of embroidery. All experiment should be undertaken freely, and attempts should constantly be made to combine design exercises with new ventures in technique.

Preparing a design and creating an embroidery are two stages in the same act of self-expression (*160*). At its simplest, the design can be a layout plan to take care of the main proportions of the finished work; again, it can be an intermediate stage between a drawing and the panel of embroidery—cut perhaps in tissue paper (*161*) to simplify, and state the main shapes of the composition. It may have been arrived at after much analytical search into subject-matter, and be so precise as to need careful tracing,★ or on the other hand, it may be a painting to which the worker refers casually (*162*). There are any number of individual ways of preparing design for embroidery. At its best it is an imaginative exercise in its own right, and very personal, providing a stimulus to the actual work as well as supplying the necessary layout (*163*). It must never be thought of as an irksome obligation, nor must embroidery be considered so separate an art form as to be independent of planned design. A plan in no way detracts from the joy of working with materials; in fact, an imaginatively painted design can be a positive inspiration in suggesting effects which might not otherwise have occurred to the worker, as shown in the *Cabbage* exercise (*61–62*).

Each worker will discover and develop her own methods of carrying out her embroideries. It has been mentioned already that works tend to develop through a series of processes; certain parts must be done first to prepare the ground for other effects. Sensible planning prevents the heart-breaking business of unpicking. To have complete delight in the work as it progresses, each stage should satisfy the embroiderer as she proceeds towards her desired effect. Knowing exactly when to stop is important. One wise summing up of good design is that 'it has nothing superfluous about it'.

★ The traditional method is by 'pricking and pouncing'. The design is traced in outline on any firm transparent paper, and pricked over a soft pad. When in position on the background, a mixture of powdered charcoal and french chalk (or ideally powdered cuttlefish bone) is dusted lightly through the holes. The outline must then be painted carefully on the material. Another method is to tack a tissue-paper tracing to the background by a fine thread, following the outline of the design, then to remove the paper by tearing, leaving the tacked outline. This is the cleaner method.

Plate 7 Celestia, *20″ × 17″. Spot composition on Chinese silk. Design inspired by growth formation of cactus. Rhythmical formations merge into one another, spiralling and radiating from the centre. Chequer-board treatment alternately emphasises and counteracts movement, suggesting new shapes. Shisha glass held in position by a system of overlapping stitches. Remainder of work in ordinary stem stitch in various thicknesses of black silk and white rayon, with yellow silk strands from the background. Direction of stitch plays a large part in finished effect of work*   *Kathleen Whyte*

160c

Stages in creating embroidery (1)
160a Drawing in gold and silver wax crayon of rocks and
weeds. Free naturally balanced arrangement

160b Embroidery in progress, on a dull grey silk ground,
with shapes of gold lamé and net. Silk stitches and laid
Japanese gold convey the gentle falling and rising rhythm
of the composition

160c Work almost complete. Much greater emphasis in
gold and drifts of small pearls. The work is shown stretched
on a frame, and surrounded by paper to isolate the exact
area of the panel, 12″ × 14″. See page 188
Joan Jeffrey, Post Diploma

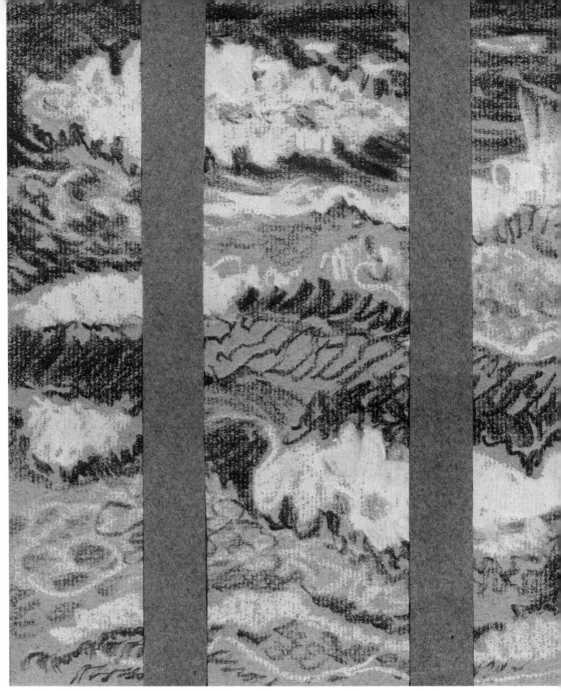

Stages in creating embroidery (2)
161a Chalk sketch of waves, with section isolated as idea
for a long panel

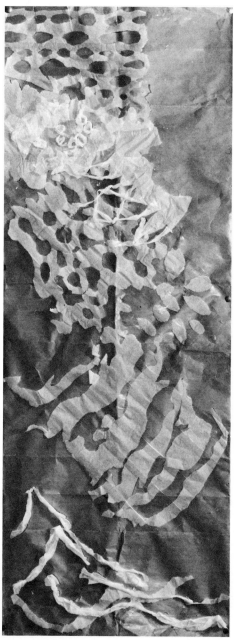

161b Design on brown paper, built up in white tissue paper

161c Embroidery, 15″ × 45″, on orange Donegal hopsack, worked in a variety of white yarns, including rough-spun linen and nylon knitting yarn. Final effect shows three lightly connected sea-shapes, worked in rosette chain, crested chain, and cable chain to create a feeling of fluidity. Both drawing and paper design could be interpreted in many other ways   Kathleen Whyte

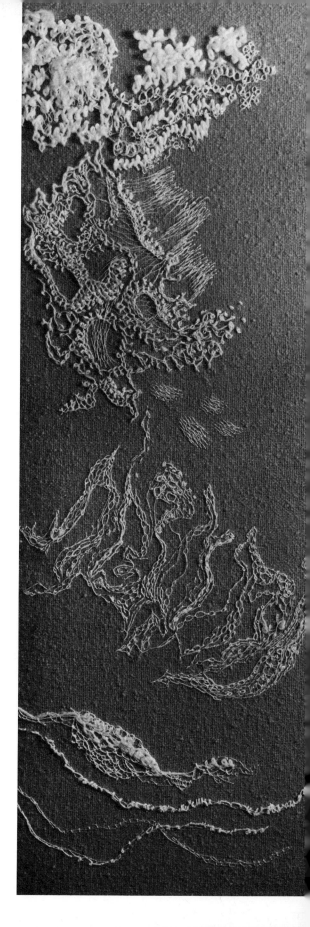

162a Sea sketches

162b Embroidery, 50″ × 36″, on cream woollen hopsack in white, pale blues, deep blues, purples, greens, and browns. 'Painterly' technique built on a foundation of Cretan and Roumanian stitches with areas of tufting and looping, and a band of heavy pattern

Susan Thom, Fourth Year 162c De

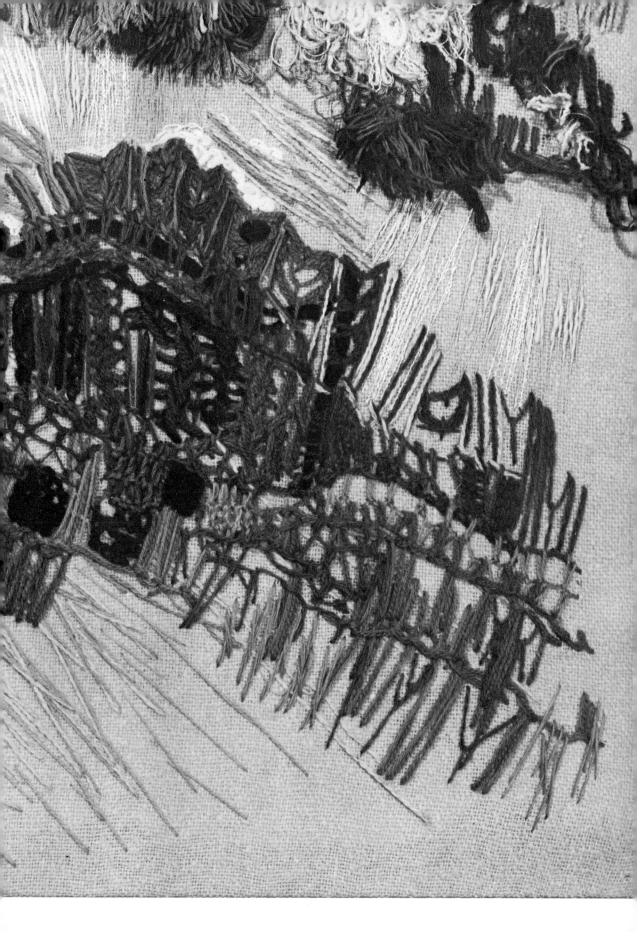

163a

163b

206

163c

Stages in creating embroidery (4). Photographs: courtesy
Facet, *Glasgow School of Art*

163a Painting of birds in an aviary

*163b Painted sketch for composition. Pattern from crowding
birds*

*163c Embroidery, 32″ × 45″, in black with vivid reds,
greens, and yellows, on a background knitted from heavy
white wool and linen. Stitchery has a stretching quality so
as not to pucker the knitted background*
Joan Jeffrey, Post Diploma

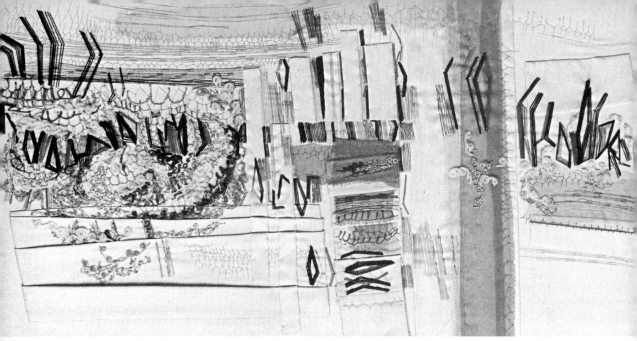

Listening to Music: Diploma Test
164a The Rite of Spring, *Stravinsky, 36″ × 18″. 'Initially I painted, keeping the theme in mind. Then I started to design in materials, taking my ideas directly from the music: growth surging, by folding material; gathering of lively people, by a background of stitchery; the Spring dance of the virgins, by swirling stitches; the old grey beards marching in, by dark jazzy triangles; and the quieter music before the victim is chosen, by centre panels of flat stitchery and material. The division of the music into two parts was brought out in the design, and throughout I tried to keep a light Spring feeling.'* Susan Thom
Background of cream silk, embroidered in creams, whites, pale greys, and dull blue-greys, in cottons, silks, and wools. Highlight colours geranium-pink and acid yellow nylon organza

Opportunity in composition

Working on a paper background, experiment with simple geometric cut shapes in a rectangle—single shapes, groups of similar shapes, two contrasting shapes, various shapes. Make—open, simple effects; full crowded effects.

Working on a material background, carry out similar experiments freely with various materials. Notice how different textures change the effects of similar shapes. Use rag-bag shapes, studying their irregularities. (Iron all shapes first.)

Divide the rectangle by lines—strings, tapes, threads—in various systems, studying the effects and resultant shapes.

Practice unit-building to change the relationship of one mass to another, as in the 'Policeman and Boys' illustration. Use cut papers and packets of adhesive spots.

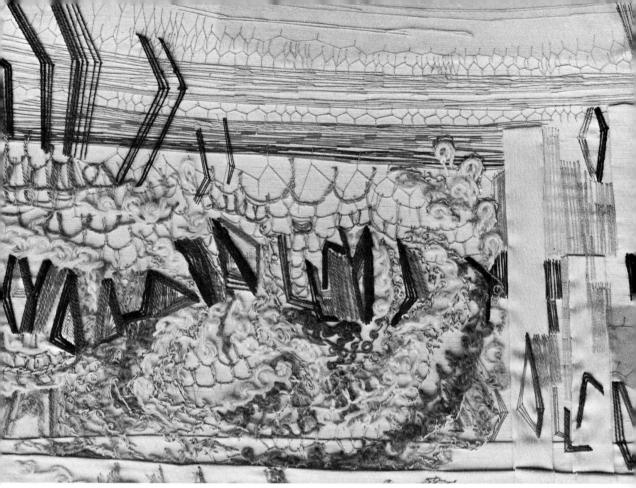

164b Detail

On different kinds of paper backgrounds, create rhythmical compositions by painting lines suggested by simple movements—water, wind, flames.

Use parts of your own sketches, forgetting their origins and seeing them as formations of lines and shapes suggesting abstract compositions (*161a*). It is a good idea to make a view-finder to help in selecting parts from a larger drawing or design. This is merely a rectangular hole cut in a fairly large piece of paper which, when laid on the drawing, isolates a small area for consideration.

Study reproductions of modern abstract paintings. They are fundamentally composed of lines and shapes. Try to discover the artist's intention within the composition as a whole.

Collect photographs from newspapers and magazines. Things seen from unusual angles suggest unusual arrangements.

Make small experimental embroideries to express your own ideas in relating materials to threads within an area. Use these as samplers for a larger work.

Make a complete and splendid embroidery!

Being ingenious

Ingenuity is a quality which should permeate the whole activity of embroidery. It has been mentioned frequently, particularly with regard to using stitches, and methods of design (*124*), but needs some further consideration. It is something to be cultivated, controlled, and when necessary curbed. It is the power of ready invention, and can show itself in manual dexterity, in the lively use of materials, and in delight at seeing analogies and discerning possibilities. Some people have a natural gift for devising intriguing methods of working, while others are less imaginative.

Many simple methods can be devised to induce and foster this quality in students. Ideas can be developed through manipulative exercises with very ordinary materials, such as paper, string, strips of wood, and drinking-straws. Questions arise: 'What can paper do?', 'What more can be done with it; and with different kinds of paper; and with string; and wood?' Each fold, each crease, each knot or cut leads on to another, each a little different, and each a pointer to the next move. Ideas link and produce chains of activity. Gradually the worker eliminates all obvious effects, and through quickened powers of invention finds that he has travelled from an easy beginning to an elaborate result.

Such exercises pave the way for working in more permanent materials, which it is part of the enterprise to discover. All kinds of braid and metal thread, large-meshed nets (*124*, *126*), leather, plastic sheeting, and cinnamoid, for instance, are materials simple in themselves but full of decorative possibilities. A word of caution is necessary here, for although it may be the intention to extend the use of these things to unconventional limits, respect for the nature of the substances must be kept in mind. Nothing must ever become so overworked as to acquire a tortured appearance. The margin between success and failure in such creations can be very narrow. It is possible to be very ingenious and at the same time create a travesty of taste—usually by unpleasant use of materials, and failure to consider the whole operation as design, with all that that implies. The classic example of misplaced ingenuity occurred when the newly invented sewing-machine was used to make meticulous copies of oil-paintings.

Richness and theatricality can sometimes be achieved by the 'heightened use' of common objects. Metal rings, washers, paper-clips, press-studs, hooks and eyes, and a host of other small things, if they have good basic shapes, can make excellent design units, their three-dimensional nature

165 Sun, *12″ diameter, detail from large panel* Phoebus
Apollo. *Glittering amalgam of circular scrap, including
metal lids, torch reflector, bracelets and scarf-pin, gaskets,
washers, pearls, sequins, buttons, jet beads, and lurex
braid—all ingeniously worked together within a car fan-
belt, edged with metal rovings* Marilyn McGregor

adding to the effect by catching the light as jewellery does. This idea is successful only when, by clever usage, these ordinary things lose their identity, and are transmuted 'into something rich and strange' (*165*). Using them at random is something to be avoided at all costs, as for example in the practice of adding a sprinkling of beads or sequins as a finishing touch to a work, like a dust of sugar on a cake. Every smallest thing has its design value, and should be considered accordingly.

There are occasions when embroidery assumes a similar role to that of jewellery, providing a setting for stones, gems, or other facets of decoration. Considerable ingenuity is needed, not only in devising methods to support the stones in position on the background, but also in creating an appropriate design to display them to the best advantage. Three examples are described in captions to *169*, *186*, and *187*.

So far, the effects suggested have been towards elaboration and richness, but it is often necessary to employ very ingenious methods to create a seemingly simple result—in Church embroidery, for instance, where padded and raised three-dimensional effects are desirable (*173*, *175*). Even the large size of a work can create problems which need to be solved, such as how to complete the embroidery in sections and join these inconspicuously. Common sense is the best guide in all such matters. Traditional usage cannot cover all contingencies, and usually the way that works will be the right way.

Ingenuity is a necessary part of all design thinking. Much modern art, noticeably 'Op Art' paintings and kinetic works display highly ingenious modes of thought. These works, by their implied or actual movement, tease the eye and intrigue the beholder. They induce a childlike quality of absorption and final delight—the fascination of ingenuity.

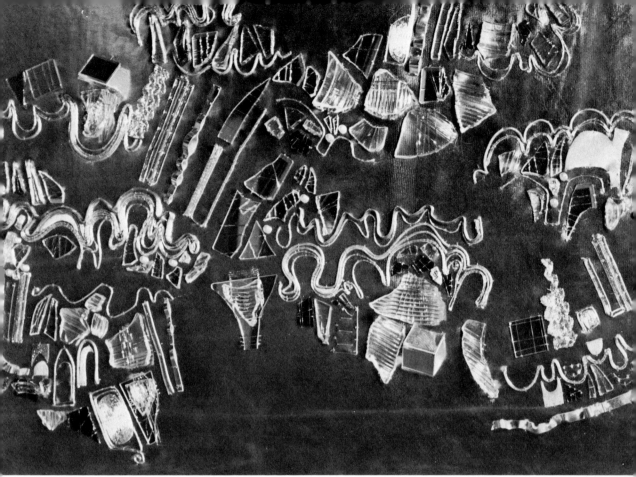

166 Reflections, *12″ × 18″. On silver plastic material, using mirror, broken glass, lurex braids, and Japanese silver*   Fiona McGeachy, Fourth Year

167 *Silver hat, theatrical, in gold plastic material, braids, sequins, beads, etc.*   Jennifer Marriot, Third Year

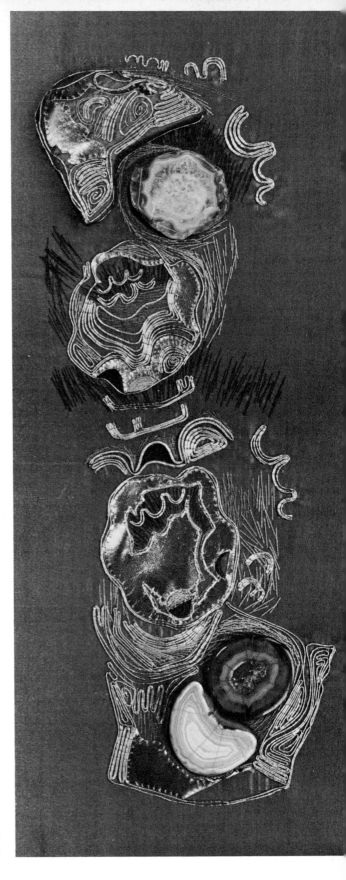

168 *Experimental cross: an attempt to escape from the rectangle. Various shapes of richly worked leather attached to a metal frame. Centre of interlaced gold holding chunks of coloured glass*
Ellen Timney, Fourth Year

169 *Design evolved as a sympathetic setting for three pieces of agate, fawn to brownish gold, 6" × 13½". Background of fine silk, shot gold, and purple. Lowest stone and shape which over-hangs upper stone built up to allow for rather heavy appearance of stones*
Susan Thom, Fourth Year

170 *Gold Cross, 18" × 40", experiment to exploit play of light on tent-shapes of gold leathers and silks, subtle variations in proportion creating elliptical effects. The background is of yellow Chinese silk and hand-woven Swedish church material in pale gold, separated by a raised panel of dull gold reverse satin* Kathleen Whyte

171 *Reversible hanging panel, 12″ square. A background covered with white buckram is pierced in geometric shapes to contain a gold cube and other suspended forms. Braids, kid, sequins, etc. are used to achieve rich textural effects*

Hannah Frew, Third Year

172 *Part of a silver pyramid, mounted on white buckram, 12″ square. Circles contrived from braid, beads, etc. decorate opposite sides, as a foil to interlacing with Japanese silver*

Joan Jeffrey, Third Year

Plate 8 Thai 3D, *silk panel, 8″ × 22″. Experiment in three-dimensional effects, to enhance colour variation and square pattern of checked Thailand silk*

Kathleen Whyte

Commissions

Commissioned work calls forth a different response in the designer from that felt when contemplating personal work for an exhibition. Conditions are no longer of her own devising but imposed from without by the wishes of other people in some particular circumstance. An imaginative approach to her client's needs can help her to accept the discipline of thinking on behalf of others as a challenge. To be asked to execute a commission brings a valuable element of reality to a designer's work, and the fortifying thought that her abilities are being used.

The worker-client relationship can be a very interesting and fruitful experience, particularly when it generates ideas. An outside point of view can provide healthy stimulus to the designer, as on the occasion when a minister, looking at an old and tired pulpit-fall adorned with anaemic lilies, exclaimed, 'That is not Easter; Easter is an explosion!' This was immediate inspiration to the designer undertaking the commission (79). Even limitations can be turned to good account and provide new starting-points for design thought.

In every case the designer must maintain her highest standards and direct her efforts to what is required, aiming to give the client more than he had thought possible or dared to hope for. On the purely practical level, when submitting designs for approval, it is wise to provide a choice. We have seen how important a matter choice is to the designer; now the client can expect to be given an opportunity to exercise his. In return, he must have complete faith in the designer's ability to carry out the work, and refrain from imposing unnecessary restrictions upon her.

Church embroidery

The first essential when undertaking a Church commission is to visit the building, in order to study its architecture and absorb its atmosphere. The environment in which the work is to be seen must be allowed to exert its influence. This atmosphere, especially in an older church, would seem to be found in the effect created by its interior proportions. Its particular feeling of space, of height and perpendicularity, the character of its walls and the width between them, all contribute to what is meant by 'the feel of the place'. If the designer is sensitive to these values, and can echo them, or take account of them by some method of contrast in her design, she will find that this is a much sounder approach to her problem than relying on the style of the furnishings and decoration as her guide. In accord with this scale of values, her design can reflect her own period and still hope to achieve an ideal timeless quality in its setting.

Designing for a new church is much simpler. New conceptions of a place of worship, new methods of construction, and new uses of proportion cannot fail to inspire pungent design. Occasionally embroidery may be chosen as the first expression of colour and richness in a fairly spartan interior. Asymmetrical design, unless it seems most appropriate to the style of the building, should be used with caution. It would require to be very telling and well placed to hold its own amidst the regularity found in most churches.

Each different denomination has its own requirements, according to its emphasis on ceremony. Some have long traditions of rich decoration, while others are essentially simple in their needs. In every case the designer is presented with the wonderful opportunity of depicting a symbol which many people will contemplate over a long period of time, and also of creating a focal point with a certain dramatic quality to read well from a distance. Her design must help to evoke a feeling of worship, and both the long and the close view be satisfied. A wealth of detail can be contained in a simple statement—an offering of rich work as of old.

Symbolism is the foundation of all Church art. It is a visual language with the power to convey beliefs and concepts of worship. Each religion has its own signs, and many in use today are very ancient in origin with universal meanings from prehistoric times. The circle is possibly the best example of this, signifying as it does the sun, life, and eternity. The present-day designer should not regard symbolism as something merely ancient and overlaid with mystery, for its very essence is that it by-passes language and outstrips time, providing her with a continuing source of subject-matter. This is not in any way to condone a tired rehash of old modes, for symbols, as well as being religiously significant, can provide the designer with an excellent array of basic design forms. The ecclesiastical cross is as simple as a road sign, and each in its own context performs the same initial function— it arrests attention. Not by their significance alone, but by the designer's manner of using them, controlled by proportion, balance, and contrast,

173 Three-dimensional silver cross on a ground of white Thailand silk, built up by degrees towards the centre, culminating in a slender gold cross, 9" square. Simple geometric shapes of silver kid mounted over felt-covered card offset the formal working of silver purl in the corners, laid Japanese silver in the large triangles, and the pattern of beads, sequins, and silver purl in the circle. Reproduction: courtesy Birmingham College of Art and Design

Hannah Frew, Post Diploma

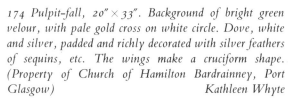

174 Pulpit-fall, 20″ × 33″. Background of bright green velour, with pale gold cross on white circle. Dove, white and silver, padded and richly decorated with silver feathers of sequins, etc. The wings make a cruciform shape. (Property of Church of Hamilton Bardrainney, Port Glasgow) Kathleen Whyte

175 Burning Bush, pulpit-fall, 22″ × 30″. Strong green-gold background, with shape built of intense flame-coloured materials and stitchery. Design a play on cross and flame. Gold leather shape cut in one piece to allow the central cross to have folded edges. (Property of Allan Park Church, Stirling) Kathleen Whyte

176 Live Coal, white pulpit-fall, 22″ × 28″, illustrating ▶ *the sixth chapter of Isaiah, and the words 'Here am I; send me'. Coal-shape built from variously textured gold leathers and transparent black materials. Upper part has a pattern of flames and lettering; lower portion has design evolved from coal, built up of shisha glass, gold kid, and vilene. A small black cross is apparent, leading to the gold cross above* Kathleen Whyte

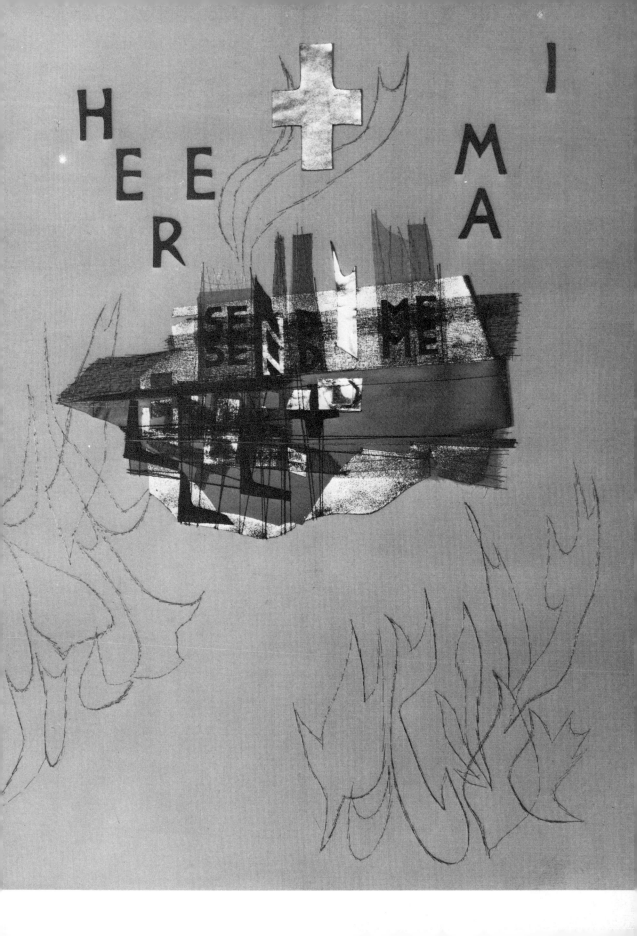

can their message be effectively conveyed. Treating them as she would any other lines and shapes, she can create feelings of simplicity and dignity, and emotions of joy and sorrow. If she has no knowledge of how to use shapes, these same religious forms can appear dreary and uninspiring. Strong simple design ensures their full impact in a church, and without this foundation no amount of dedicated work and skill in execution, be it in embroidery or any other art, will have its full value.

The Church presents embroidery with a wonderful opportunity. All the possibilities for display of colour and texture in materials, ingenious devising to create depth and highlight, and the exploiting of rich techniques can be brought into play.

Colour creates a mood, and its imaginative use gives added expression to the content of a design. Liturgical colour with its symbolic significance may dictate a particular shade, or an existing scheme of church decoration may limit the range of choice, but, as has already been shown, exciting schemes of colour can be developed from any starting-point.

Fabrics are chosen for their quality and effect. They should be the best available consistent with the designer's intention regarding colour and surface appearance. There are excellent background materials to be had in liturgical colours, but these need not be adhered to unless specifically desired. All the wide range of fabrics is at the worker's disposal, and here as in other fields imaginative choice plays its part. The impact of much Church embroidery depends on the bold use of shape. When applying material shapes to a background, methods of workmanship must be strong and finished to wear well, but the quality of outline which different types of application present in the finished design must be kept in mind. Some edges require hard definition while others merge softly, and where special accent is desired ornate effects can be used. Dramatic qualities of highlight and shadow greatly enhance any work to be viewed from a distance. In embroidery these effects can be achieved by the use of rich materials such as leathers, lurex fabrics, and cloth of gold. Their effectiveness is further enhanced by padding and building up on card or balsa-wood foundations to create variety in surface levels. Shapes are usually prepared individually and applied to the work at the right stage of its development. Several instances of such treatment are illustrated, and attention is directed to *136*,

170, 173 in particular, and other examples in this section of the book. Ingenious experiment plays a large part in how the worker evolves ideas for three-dimensional effects. The only advice given is very obvious: the plainer a surface is kept the more it catches the light. It is wise to keep studying the prepared facets for light effects before fixing them finally in position.

The foundation of all intricate detail and rich effect in ecclesiastical embroidery is undoubtedly the practice of laying Japanese gold thread, with all its attendant techniques. This very important subject has merely been touched on, when its basic ideas were outlined as an area for experiment. The reader is advised to study the authoritative works on the subject listed at the end of this book, and urged to spend some time in learning and practising before attempting any elaborate use of gold on an important work.

Church embroidery is a large subject which expands with experiment and practice, but there is no mystique about it. All facets of design are relevant to it, and although its ultimate image is one of rich elaboration of detail, simplicity of statement is its ideal.

177b Detail

◀ *177a* Creation, *pulpit-fall, 18″ × 34″, on red hand-woven ecclesiastical silk. Circle, cross, and bar are easily read from a distance. Details within the circle, representing the elements, humanity, and animal and plant life, appear like insets in primitive jewellery. (Property of St Martin's Church, Port Glasgow)* Kathleen Whyte

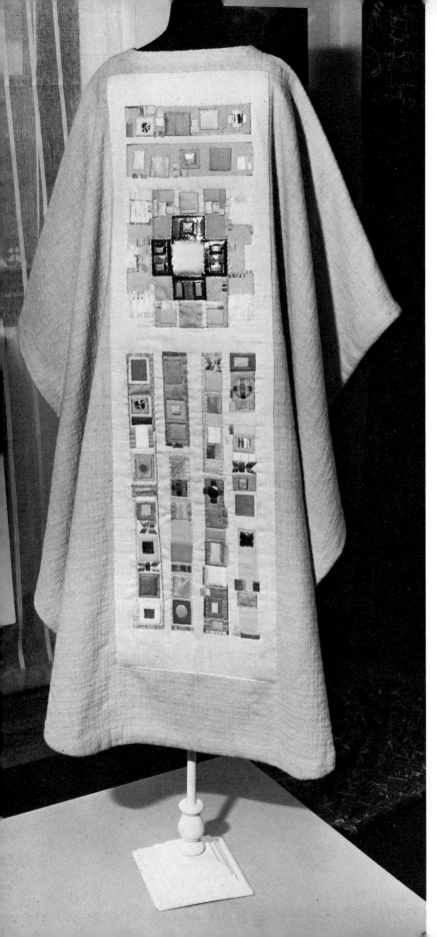

178 Chasuble, on hand-woven white woollen fabric. Embroidery on a panel of white silk, using patches of material, plastic, and leather, in yellows, golds, pinks, and other light colours, creates a very simple architectural effect. Cross, of gold kid has insets of padded satin
Anna McCann, Post Diploma

179 Banner, 28″ × 48″. The figure of St Michael is a simple column of intricate patchwork in rich red materials, with the pattern growing naturally into a pectoral cross. Wings formed of elliptical shapes of pale gold and orange-pink. The devil is green and black.
Photograph : courtesy Glasgow Herald
Veronica Togneri

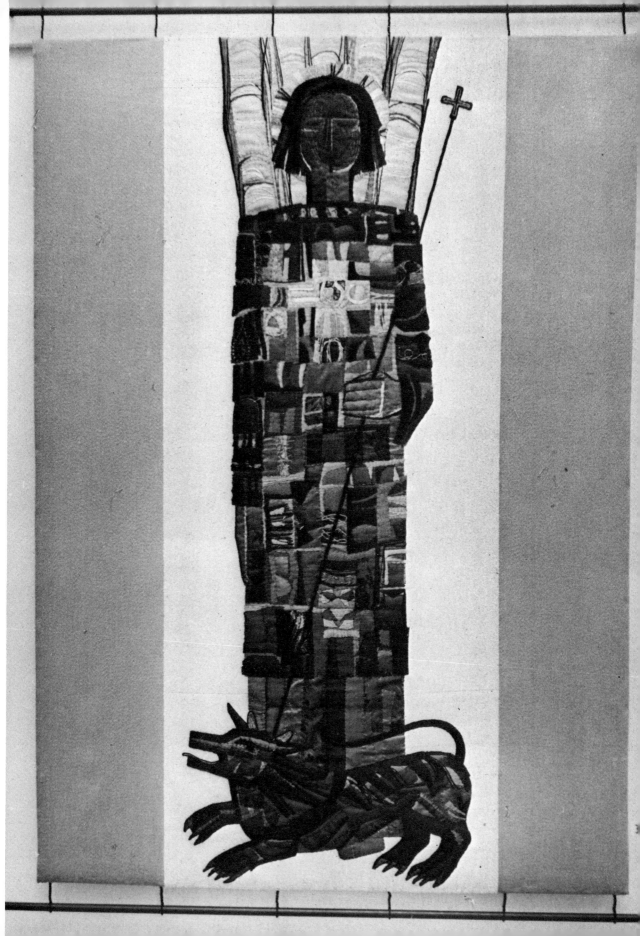

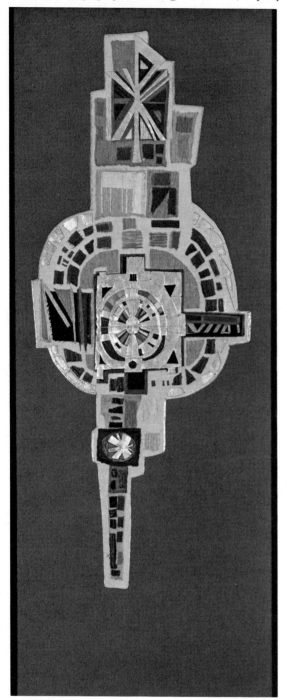

180 *Red silk ground, 16″ × 34″. Motif based on a thistle, in pink Thailand silk with a mosaic effect of reds, blues, and purples, is in materials and stitchery. The Chi Rho, the central motif of cross, circle, and square, and the small St Andrew's Cross are of gold kid, lashed in position with Japanese gold*   Jan Machesney, Fourth Year

181 *Purple silk background, 16″ × 34″. Heavy, sad cross, built in facets of various gold and copper leathers and materials. Centre, a pyramid of laid Japanese gold. Dove-shape can be discerned flying upwards. Very severe crown of thorns in silver kid*

Fiona MacCallum, Post Diploma

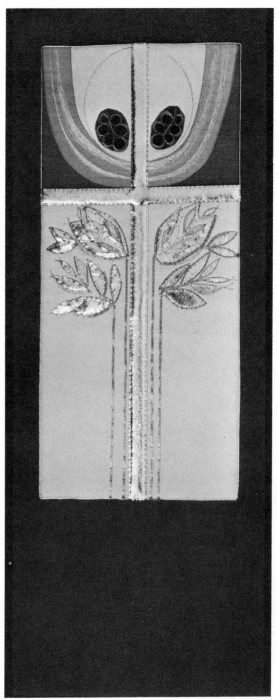

182 White corded silk background, 16″ × 34″. Cross and circle motif, in contrasting gold leathers with a blue background, appears suspended on a slender gold rod from a bar of gold with three circles, enclosing corn, dove, and fish symbols   *Janet Boyd, Fourth Year*

183 On a green background, a panel of white silk is quartered by a slender cross of gold, 16″ × 34″. Upper portion shows a chalice shape, containing a white circle and vine motifs, against a pale mauve silk background; in the lower part heavy heads of corn rise on slender stems, worked in gold leather and laid work

Janet Boyd, Fourth Year

184 Last Supper, *12″ × 7″. On padded purple silk, in a recessed frame. The whole motif is a truncated cross. The figure of Christ is treated as a symbol, while the Apostles form a pattern of intensely human faces. Judas, on the extreme right, is distinguished by an ugly hand. Worked in laid gold, appliqué, and silk embroidery*

Kathleen Whyte

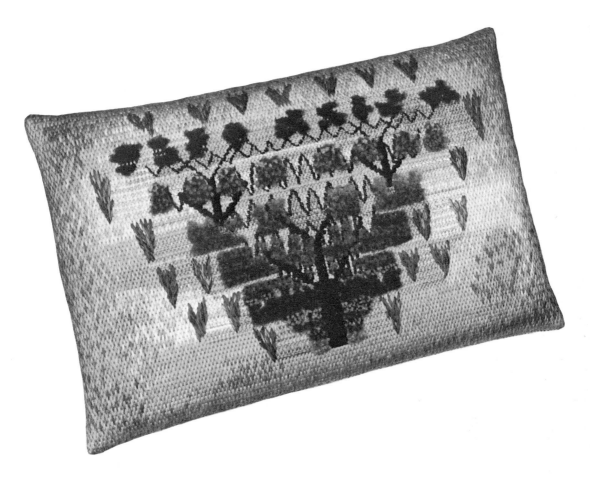

185 Burning Bush, *kneeler. Worked on canvas background, in shadings of flame colour. Bush has a cross formation at the base, with tufting in dull, blue-brown cinder colours, and is surrounded by cerise and petunia-coloured flames. (Property of the Victoria and Albert Museum, London)* Kathleen Whyte

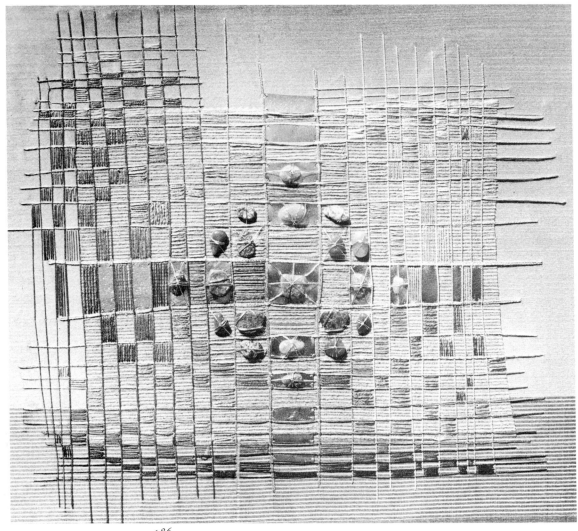

186

Embroidery for special occasions

Making an embroidery as a gift is a special experience, giving the worker a sense of intimate purpose. Her imagination can be directed solely to giving pleasure to the recipient. Her work may be used to mark an official occasion or to convey personal regard. The idea of embroidery, the whole of it with all its possibilities, as a gift to everyone who cares to participate in its struggles and delights would seem to be the right note on which to end this book.

186 Iona, *a personal souvenir, 20″ square. The island of Iona lies off the west coast of Scotland. St Columba landed there in the sixth century, bringing Christianity. Sea-polished pebbles of 'Iona green stone' (green serpentine) are found on the beaches on the south side of the island. They vary from translucent olive-umber to yellow-green, and dull green marbled with white. The background of the panel, representing the sea, is of clear turquoise blue silk with a border shading into grey. An oblong of corded silk in greenish grey, like the stones, forms the island. On this foundation threads, chosen for colour and tone, trace some-thing akin to the warp and weft of an old weaving pattern, concentrating in the centre with lines of silver, which create a framework for pieces of silver kid and the stones to form a Celtic cross. The island's characteristic colours select and fill other shapes, creating a gentle rhythm—purple at the foot for seaweed under the water, soft green for the grass at the left, rising to strong ocean-blues beyond the island; pale greenish yellows lead to pure white sands. Photograph: Mr Wesley Bowman, Chicago. (Property of Dr and Mrs David Newton Danforth, Chicago)* Kathleen Whyte

187 Embroidered stole for official presentation. Commis-*sioned by the Corporation of Dundee, for presentation to Her Majesty, Queen Elizabeth, the Queen Mother, on the occasion of her declaring open the road bridge over the River Tay. An intriguing condition was that the design should feature a quantity of the very lovely mussel pearls found in the river. Forty of these were used, ranging in size from small seeds to boutons of three-eighths of an inch in diameter, some perfect in shape, others irregular, and with colours and lustres varying from clear pinks, through all the pearl shades to gold and deep mauve. The stole, of pure silk in cream and gold, hand-woven by Ursula Brook, has the embroidery placed at the lower right when worn. The river is represented by a band of tissue-like embroidery in fine gold, and the bridge spanning it appears somewhat like a Celtic clasp, with the pearls in swirling foam cascading beneath it. The design includes three emblems (these too were obligatory)—a crowned heart for the County of Angus, a pot of lilies for the City of Dundee, and a knight on a charger for Fife, which lies to the south of the river. (Property of Queen Elizabeth, the Queen Mother)* Kathleen Whyte

Books for reference and further study

Dictionary of Embroidery Stitches   Mary Thomas   Hodder and Stoughton

Samplers and Stitches   Mrs A Christie   Batsford

Embroidery Stitches   Barbara Snook   Batsford 1963

100 Embroidery Stitches   J & P Coats Ltd

Anchor Manual of Needlework   J & P Coats Ltd   Batsford 1958

Patchwork   Averil Colby   Batsford 1958

Traditional Quilting   Mavis Fitzrandolph   Batsford   (out of print)

Ecclesiastical Embroidery   Beryl Dean   Batsford 1958

Ideas for Church Embroidery   Beryl Dean   Batsford 1968

Metal Thread Embroidery   Barbara Dawson   Batsford 1968

The Flowerers   Margaret Swain   Chambers   (out of print)

English Historical Embroidery   Barbara Snook   Batsford 1960   (out of print)

The Bayeux Tapestry   Norman Denny and Josephine Pelman-Sankey
    Collins 1966

Index